POLITICALLY INCORRECT ANSWERS TO AMERICA'S BURNING ISSUES:

FROM THE BOOK WHICH CANNOT LIE

DR. BILL BENNETT

Unless otherwise indicated, all Scripture quotations are taken from the *New King James Version* 1979, 1980, 1982 by Thomas Nelson, Inc.

Scriptures marked (*KJV*) are taken from the *King James Version* of the Bible.

Scripture quotations marked (*NIV*) are taken from the *Holy Bible: New International Version®*. NIV®. Copyright © 1973, 1978, 1984 by International Bible Society. Used by permission of Zondervan Publishing House. All rights reserved.

Scriptures marked (*Phillips*) are taken from J.B. Phillips *The New Testament in Modern English,* New York: MacMillan Publishing Company, 1958, 1959, 1960, 1972.

Politically Incorrect Answers to Today's Burning Issues
Copyright © 2008 by Dr. Bill Bennett
104 King Arthur Drive
Wilmington, NC 28403

PRINTED BY:

2145 WRIGHTSVILLE AVENUE
WILMINGTON, NC 28403
VOICE/FAX: 910.763.5599

Printed in the United States of America.
All rights reserved under International Copyright Law.
Contents and/or cover may not be reproduced in whole or in part in any form without the express written consent of the Publisher.

Acknowledgements and Salutations:

I wish to salute some very special persons who have shaped my life profoundly and enriched my ministry immeasurably…

First, I wish to acknowledge my profound thanks to my Administrative Assistant, Mrs. Elsie Johnson, whom I call Ms. "E", who spent endless hours in typing and re-typing the manuscript and researching the sources; also to my precious granddaughter, Angela, whom I call my "beautiful and brilliant little angel", who proved from a scientific viewpoint, that life begins at conception; also I wish to acknowledge my profound appreciation for the very insightful chapters written by two young scholars and my former students, Dr. Paul Brewster, (chapter 2) and Dr. Bryan Sims, (chapter 12).

I salute my bride of 56 years, Doris Faye, the greatest Christian I have ever known. Her favorite song is "I'd Rather Have Jesus," and she has lived out this song while following me to the ends of the earth and giving me three remarkable Bennetts: Dr. Bill, Jr., Philip Judson, and David Palmer.

I salute my precious Mom, who sanctified me in her womb, and instilled in me the principle that "it's a sin to make a "C" in life when you are capable of making an "A," and you can do the latter." I only wished my professors at Duke and Wake Forest Universities had believed this.

I salute my dear Dad, a powerful proclaimer of the "whole" gospel, teaching me the requirement of holiness and the Spirit-filled life, before many Baptists discovered these truths were found in the Bible.

I salute Mary Elizabeth Stanton, high school teacher, who enabled me to understand English grammar, equipping me to enter and succeed in the greatest institutions of higher learning in the world.

I salute my Professor Forest Clontz, of whom I was assistant in college, who required me to enlarge my vocabulary, equipping me to write myriads of research papers in graduate school, including my doctrinal dissertation.

I salute David Burton, a huge lover and supporter of MMM and a faithful friend who has stuck closer than a brother for a generation.

I salute "Ma" Becton, who became my mother away from home in college.

I salute Calvary Baptist Church, Durham, N. C., my first pastorate, for loving and forgiving me of my youthful foibles and predicting I would be Billy Graham's successor, which I foolishly believed until my second Deacon's meeting.

I salute Mrs. Janey Spencer, who stood by my side for almost twenty years, as I shouldered the responsibilities of a large congregation, the First Baptist Church, Fort Smith, Arkansas. She protected me from my enemies and ingratiated me to my friends.

I salute Mrs. Ann Curtis, who labored by my side for almost twenty years, enabling me to assemble and teach one of the largest Bible classes in America and to train 3000 persons to share their faith, using the EE model.

I salute the growing company of guys across the world, both lay and clerical, whom I have mentored and who have been conformed into Christ's image by Internalizing the Word of God.

I salute my dear brother and friend, Nathan Sanders, who has been the premier supporter of MMM. Int'l.

I salute Brother Bob Kester, generous Christian layman, who has steadily encouraged me and supported our ministries since 1995.

Table of Contents

A 'Politically Incorrect' Word From 'Dr. B'

1. Is Jesus the Only Way to Heaven?...................9
2. What is the Truth About Truth? 19
3. Can a Person Who Commits Suicide go to Heaven?...24
4. Hell: A State of Mind or Real Estate?.........................31
5. Same Sex Marriage: Let the Bible Speak..................42
6. Abortion: Let Scripture and Science Speak...............50
7. The Greatest Heresy Plaguing Evangelicals Today......62
8. Why the War Against Christianity?..............................80
9. The 5 Myths About Homosexuality.........................97
10. The Place for Women in the Local Church..............107
11. Is it Scriptural to Address God as Mother?................127
12. Why does a Good God Allow Good People to Suffer?..137
13. Who killed Jesus?..156

A 'POLITICALLY INCORRECT' WORD FROM 'DR. B'

The term "politically correct" is all the buzz in today's culture. I make no claim to any special insight on political correctness. However, the very words "politically correct" furnish the clue that points to its meaning.

"Political" has been defined as *the art of compromise.* "Correct" in this context means *that which is right in the eyes of sinful and self-serving human beings.* The two words combined create the following meaning: The correct way to live is to think and conform to the standards of this evil world. This includes not only conforming to these standards, but also accepting and never condemning the views of others, no matter how much those views violate the truth and your own convictions.

The words "politically correct" do not appear in the Bible. However, the Bible warns of the danger of such a world view. Twice the Bible asserts, "There is a way that seems right to a man [the "politically correct" way], but its end is the way of death" (Proverbs 14:12; Proverbs 16:25). In the New Testament the Apostle Paul cogently warns believers to avoid the false thinking of the secular world. "Beware lest any man spoil you through philosophy and vain deceit, after the tradition of men, after the rudiments of the world, and not after Christ" (Col. 2:8).

Politically correct ways of thinking and acting may seem right, but according to God's Word, they are totally wrong and ultimately destructive. Why do men pursue such a destructive course? Jesus answers with these words: "And this is the judgment, that the light has come into the world, and men loved darkness rather than light, because their deeds were evil" (John 3:19).

Dr. Allan Moseley, Dean at Southeastern Baptist Theological Seminary, wrote a superb book entitled *Thinking Against the Grain.* In this book, Dr. Moseley shows that political incorrectness is going against the grain of the speech and action of the body politic. In a recent email to me, Dr. Moseley further expounds on the meaning of political correctness with these words:

> In order to be "politically correct," one must make a commitment to conform one's speech and actions to the opinions of the body politic, as far as that is possible. For a Christian, such a commitment is impossible. We have a prior commitment conformity to the will of God as revealed in the Scriptures. Unfortunately, this basic Christian commitment makes Christians politically incorrect in the West these days. Media representatives remind everyone of this regularly when they warn of how dangerous and extreme are the views of Bible-believing Christians. No matter. Christians have been politically incorrect for a long time; we take our marching orders from the Word of the Sovereign God, not from a politician.

The Church was birthed in political incorrectness, and in its orthodox expression, has adhered to this viewpoint through the ages, often suffering persecution for its stance. For 250 years in the Roman Empire, it was politically correct to worship Caesar and offer incense to the gods of Rome, and it was politically *in*correct to worship Jesus. Yet Christians continued to worship Jesus, refusing to bow to Caesar, and Christianity flourished in that environment of opposition, even though persecuted.

The entire politically correct movement rises and falls on a twisted redefinition of the word "tolerance." Whereas tolerance once meant allowing people the space to have their own foibles and sins, now tolerance has been redefined to mean that we must applaud, legalize, and pander to the basest behaviors and values. Our failure to do so with certain "hot-button" issues and groups means that we become politically incorrect.

If we are indeed nearing Jesus' "Glorious Appearing," and if the Bible is anything like an accurate roadmap pointing toward what is to come, then we as Christians must expect pressure to continue to mount regarding our political incorrectness. More and more, we will be called upon to choose:

- Do we speak the truth and subsequently suffer increasingly harsh persecution?
- Or do we suppress the truth and acquiesce to the politically correct policy on a particular issue?

This was the choice Martin Luther faced at the Diet of Worms (1521), but when given the latter option, he declared that such a choice was not "safe." Imagine the significance of this! When commanded to disown his politically incorrect writings, Luther declared it was not safe to do so knowing that failing to recant was almost certain to make a martyr out of him.

In light of the above discussion, one must conclude that political correctness is a worldview that is drastically contrary to God's truth as revealed in the Holy Scriptures. It is also totally antithetical to the teachings of Jesus Christ, the Son of God, and repugnant to Christian doctrine and behavior. God commands us through the Apostle Paul, "Don't let the world around you squeeze you into its own mold, but let God re-make you so that your whole attitude of mind is changed" (Romans 12:2 *Phillips*).

It is my hope and prayer that the messages to follow will cause you to evaluate how biblical truths intersects with some of the burning issues in today's culture.

Dr. Bill Bennett

1
IS JESUS THE ONLY WAY TO HEAVEN?

Evangelicalism has always been a diverse movement. It has encompassed every entity from hard-nosed fundamentalists like J. Frank Norris and Bob Jones (1930-1950) to the Jesus People (1960's – 70's). But every expression of evangelicalism has had one distinctive feature until recently: They all believed that Jesus Christ, the Son of God, is the only way to God and Heaven.

Forty years ago, the "One Way Sign" – the index finger held high- became a popular icon. "One Way" bumper stickers and lapel pins were seen everywhere. "One Way" slogans were the identifying "catchphrases" of all Evangelicals – Baptomethopaliancongrepresbygationalists.

However, the Evangelical movement is no longer united on this issue. Two viewpoints have risen to challenge this position:
- (1) Those who are convinced that people of all faiths will be in heaven, not just those who have trusted Jesus Christ.
- (2) The cowardly who, though they profess to be conservatives, are embarrassed to proclaim the exclusivity of the gospel, the "One Way" to God and Heaven, when pluralism and tolerance are deemed cardinal virtues in western cultures.[1]

Why has this dramatic shift occurred in Evangelical thought? Several factors have undoubtedly produced it:

1. **The Rejection of the Authority of the Bible**. The source of the "One Way" theology is the Holy Scriptures, and when the absolute authority of the Bible is denied, the doctrine of the "One Way" falls with that viewpoint.

---

[1] See John McArthur, Why One Way, W Publishing Group, 2002, pp. vii-viii.

2. **The Rise of Post Modernism**. Modernism reigned in most of the 20th century, teaching that science is the only pathway to truth. Now Post Modernism has arisen to deny this view-point, insisting that there is no such thing as absolute, objective, universal truth. Thus by Post Modern thought truth is subjectively determined by each person. Thus truth is nothing more than one's opinion. So to say that Jesus is the only way to God is regarded by many moderns as absolutely unacceptable, insulting, even idiotic, and therefore unbinding on enlightened humankind.

3. **The Replacement of Reality by Ridiculous Tolerance**. In a Post-Modern culture, tolerance is the dominant feature. The word "tolerance" used to mean respecting people and treating them kindly; but in Post-Modern thought tolerance means we must never regard anyone else's opinion as wrong. To tell anyone that Jesus is the only way to God is totally unacceptable and even the unpardonable sin.

4. **The Refusal of Many Pastors to Preach their Convictions**. I asked Dr. Al Mohler, President of Southern Baptist Theological Seminary this question: "How would you describe Southern Baptist preaching today?" Without hesitation, he replied, "Most Southern Baptist preachers and pastors have lost their 'nerve' to preach the whole counsel of God, including the truth that Jesus Christ is the one an only way to God." Dr. James Kennedy used to say that "Three hundred thousand pulpits in America are silent on the issues of abortion, same-sex marriages, homo-sexuality."

5. **The "Relevance Craze" Sweeping the Nation**. Many religious leaders are so desperate to be relevant and fashionable that they are willing to sacrifice truth or dilute it to mean nothing, failing to see that they are in fact sacrificing the saving gospel on a

false premise. Dr. John McArthur writes a scathing word at this point, "Preachers are terrified that the offense of the gospel might turn someone against them; so they deliberately omit the parts of the message the world might not like.

Evangelicalism seems to have been hijacked by legions of carnal spin-doctors, who are trying their best to convince the world that the church can be just as inclusive, pluralistic, and broad-minded as the most politically-correct worldling.

The quest for the world's approval is nothing less than spiritual harlotry. In fact, that is precisely the imagery the apostle James used to describe it. He wrote, 'Adulterers and adulteresses! Do you not know that friendship with the world is enmity with God? Whoever therefore wants to be a friend of the world makes himself an enemy of God' (James 4:4)."[2]

6. **The Results of Cultural Pressure:** "One Way" is despised by the mainstream media and liberal elites. Just as with woman's roles and homosexuality, it is another case of the church compromising to culture.

Having rejected the "One Way" Gospel, modern man has now posited three main approaches to get around the "One Way" approach:

(1) **Universalism** – Another name for Universalism is pluralism, which holds there are many ways, even unlimited number to God and everyone will eventually be saved and reach heaven. This heresy goes back as far as Origen in the second century (185-254 AD.). This position is popular with liberal theologians and New Age followers. This view is strongly espoused by John Hicks in these words: "Most New Testament scholars today do not believe that Jesus,

---

[2] Ibid, pp. 12

the historical individual, claimed to be God incarnate. The old exclusivist view that only Christians are saved has been abandoned by the majority of Christian theologians and church leaders."[3] Hicks has greatly exaggerated the extent of Universalism, but the fact that Universalism or Pluralism is rife in our times cannot be denied. Some years ago, I believe about 2000, Dr. Paige Patterson, Jerry Falwell, and I were having lunch on the campus of SEBTS, and I asked these brothers this question, "What do you think is the greatest danger Southern Baptist's will be facing in the years to come?" They both said, "Universalism." I myself and other evangelicals have thought, that there is but a short step from "Easy Believism,"[4] (which is widespread in Evangelical churches today), to Universalism.

(2) **Inclusivism** – Adherents of this view claim that Jesus is the only Savior, but that it is possible for Jesus to save people even though they have never personally trusted Him for salvation. This view amounts to this: People can receive salvation by responding to God's revelation in nature and conscience (general revelation), or even through other world religions. Other religions may have an imperfect understanding of the one true God, but the truth they teach is adequate to save them. Roman Catholic Karl Rahner says such persons should be recognized as "anonymous Christians" because of their good deeds. Dr. Clark Pinnock, once a flaming fundamentalist and a man I knew personally and admired greatly, has come to embrace the "inclusivist" position. He writes, "According to Acts 4:12, ...Jesus has done a unique work for the human race, the good news of which needs to be preached to

---

[3] World Faiths Encounter, March 2001, pp. 3-11.
[4] The wide spread teaching that all one needs to do to get saved is to believe in his head that Jesus died for his sin, to confess this fact in a prayer, say the same before a congregation, be immersed in water and that makes a person a Christian.

the whole world. But this uniqueness does not entail exclusivity."⁵

(3) **Annihilationism** – the view that the wicked will be ultimately exterminated and cease to exist. Dr. J. W. Stott and Dr. Clark Pinnock, once highly respected in evangelical circles, espouse this view point.⁶

EXCLUSIVISM –(The One-Way) This is the Biblical and True Position

This position holds that salvation comes only through a personal trust in Jesus Christ as Lord and Savior. "Exclusivism affirms the absolute uniqueness and finality of God's revelation in Jesus. He alone is the Savior, the definitive, and ultimate expression of divine truth. Only in Him can people be saved. God would not have sent His only Son to die on a cross if He could have saved us another way. The cross of Christ is God's greatest testimony that Jesus is the exclusive way to the Father."⁷ Exclusivism has been held by the historic church, both Catholic and Protestant, for most of its history. The great Princeton theologian, Benjamin Warfield, in The Person and Work of Christ, affirms the uniqueness of Jesus in cogent language. He wrote, "Christ is Christianity itself; He stands not outside of it but in its center; without His name, person and work, there is no Christianity left. In a word, Christ does not point out the way to salvation; He is the Way itself."⁸

Finally, the question remains, what is our basis for believing that Jesus Christ is the one and only way to God and to heaven? Our basis lies in the repeated teaching of the Holy Scripture, especially the New Testament. When

---

⁵ Quoted in Daniel Akin, Discovering the Biblical Jesus, Nashville, Tennessee: Life Press, 2003, p. 90.
⁶ Al Mohler, Hell Under Fire, Grand Rapids, Michigan: Zondervan, p. 30
⁷ Akin, Ibid. p. 91
⁸ Benjamin B. Warfield, The Person and Work of Christ, p.319.

we search the New Testament we find that all the major writers declare categorically, and with no ambiguity, that Jesus is the one and only way to God and to heaven:

1. **Jesus Himself, the Son of God**, says in John 14:6 that He is the only way to the Father. Verse 6 literally begins with the assertion, "I Myself am the Way." Jesus used an intensive pronoun to stress that He and He alone is the way, the truth, the Life. The article is prominently placed before the three words: *Ho Hodos* (way), *Ho Aletheia* (truth), and *Ho Zoe* (life). Without the Way, there is no going; without the truth, there is no knowing; and without the Life, there is no Living. Hallelujah what a Savior. Not only did Jesus declare "He is the Way …to the Father." But He reinforced this truth when He went on to say, "No one comes to the Father except through me" (John 14:6) and to know Him was to know the Father (John 14:7). To know Jesus is to know God, and to see Jesus is to see the Father (John 14:9).

2. **The Apostle Peter, Chief of the Apostles**, said that Jesus is the way. Peter is defending himself before the Sanhedrin who asked him, "By what power or by what Name have you done this?" "Then Peter, filled with the Holy Spirit, said to them, "Rulers of the people and elders of Israel: If we this day are judged for a good deed *done* to a helpless man, by what means he has been made well, let it be known to you all, and to all the people of Israel, that by the name of Jesus Christ of Nazareth, whom you crucified, whom God raised from the dead, by Him this man

stands here before you whole. This is the *'stone which was rejected by you builders, which has become the chief cornerstone.* <u>Nor is there salvation in any other, for there is no other name under heaven given among men by which we must be saved.</u> Now when they saw the boldness of Peter and John, and perceived that they were uneducated and untrained men, they marveled. And they realized that they had been with Jesus" (Acts 4:8-13).

3. **The Apostle Paul** said that Jesus is the only way. Instructing young Timothy, Paul states that God wants everyone to be saved and come to knowledge of the truth (1 Tim. 2:4). Then Peter points out that there is only one way humankind can enter into the presence of a holy God – through the "one God and one mediator between God and man, the man Christ Jesus" (1 Tim. 2:5). God's invitation is universal, but His salvation is specific and exclusive. It is only through His Son, Jesus, and in no other (1 John 5:12; Romans 10:9-15).

4. **The Apostle John** said that Jesus is the Only Way. By quoting the very words of Jesus, as stated above in John 14:6-9, the beloved apostle clearly believed and affirmed that Jesus alone is the only way to God and heaven. 1 John 5:12 teaches the same truth.

5. **The Historic Church** for almost 2000 years, both Protestant and Catholic, has confessed that Jesus is the only Savior, the only way to God and heaven. Examinations of the great creeds of Christendom and the confessions of individual denomi-

nations have affirmed Jesus Christ as the only way to be saved. The departure from this belief has taken place within the last two generations among evangelicals.

There still remains a vital question about the "One Way":

Why One Way?

To answer this question we have to look at the history of human kind. Adam and Eve were created by God in His own image, in true holiness and righteousness. But they deliberately disobeyed God, and immediately they died spiritually, which ultimately brought physical death also (Gen. 2:17). Thus man's sin separated him from a holy God. However, God, because of "His great love wherewith He loved us," (Ephes. 2:4) sent His One and only begotten (*monogenes*, the only one of His kind) to die for two basic reasons:

    1. The sinfulness of man, and
    2. The holiness of God.

Romans 3:23 states, "All have sinned and fallen short of the glory of God." But by Jesus substituting Himself on the cross, God Himself demonstrated His righteousness so that He (God) would be righteous and holy and declare as righteous all who believed in Jesus (Romans 3:24). The glorious result being, "We are freely justified (declared righteous) by His grace (free gift) through the redemption that is in Christ Jesus."

Thus we may confidently conclude that Jesus is the One and Only Way to God because God the Father appointed Him to be and no one else. In fact, Jesus is the only One who ever qualified to be our Savior, since He, the God man, was the only person ever to live without sin. As the writer of Hebrews says, "Therefore He is also able to save to the uttermost those who come to God through Him, since He always lives to make intercession for them. *For such a High Priest was fitting for us, who is* holy, harmless, undefiled, separate from sinners, and has become higher than the heavens" (Hebrews 7:25-26)

The best-known verse in all the Bible is John 3:16, which succinctly states the truth of all I am attempted to say above. "God loved the world in this way: He gave His One and Only Son, so that everyone who believes in Him will not perish but have eternal life." Then John re-enforces this truth by stating further, "God did not send His Son into the world to judge the world, but that the world through Him might be saved. Anyone who believes in Him is not judged, but anyone who does not believe is already judged, because he has not believed in the name of the One and Only Son of God" (John 3:17-18).

Conclusion

Why would anyone seek another way than the way God has provided? Jesus answers this question in John 3:18-19, "He who believes in Him is not condemned; but he who does not believe is condemned already, because he has not believed in the name of the only begotten Son of God. And this is the condemnation, that the light has come into the world, and men loved darkness rather than light, because their deeds were evil." Man's rejection of Christ is not an intellectual problem but a moral one. In a word, man does not want to humble his heart and bring himself under the Lordship of Jesus Christ. Chuck Colson has so aptly stated, "It's obvious why Eastern religion is such an attractive form of salvation for a post-Christian culture. It soothes the ego by pronouncing the individual divine, and it gives a gratifying sense of 'spirituality' without making any demands in terms of doctrine of ethical living."[9] The religions of this world differ in teachings and rituals, but all of them have one thing in common: they teach salvation by good works, human merit or personal accomplishments. Only does the atoning death of Jesus Christ on the cross offer the good news of salvation by grace through faith through the accomplishments of the One and Only who paid in full the price of sin as our Mediator, Savior, Lord and coming King. The wise will heed the warning of Solomon, "There is a way that seems right to man, but in the end it leads to death" (Prov. 14:12; Prov. 16:25). Be sure you have or will choose the only way to eternal life – the Lord Jesus Christ."

---

[9] Chuck Colson, How Should We Then Live, p. 125.

2
"The Truth about Truth"
By Dr. Paul Brewster – Ph.D in Theology

When historians look over their shoulders at the preceding march of time, they often key in on one big idea to pigeonhole entire generations. For example, textbooks on ancient history are commonly filled with references to "The Iron Age." What is meant is that advances in metallurgy made at that time were very significant in terms of explaining the progress and development of civilization. Closer to our own era, we also find historians speaking of the "Modern Age." In that moniker, "modern" means far more than simply "new." Rather, it denotes a certain way of looking at the world—what philosophers love to call by its German name, *weltanschauung*. In America, we call it simply "worldview." As a worldview, modernism was characterized by a strong belief in the power of human reason to understand and explain all reality. It was also optimistic about the possibility of human progress on any number of fronts if only the truth about each subject area could be discovered and applied. The quest for truth became preeminent. The characteristic pre-modern confidence in divine revelation gave way to greater and greater trust in the powers of human reasoning.

Admittedly, the modern enterprise has made good on many of its endeavors, especially making vast strides in technologies of all descriptions. Diseases that once terrorized entire populations have literally been eliminated. Oceans which were all but insuperable barriers to travel can now be crossed in a matter of hours. In other fields, however, modernism was not nearly as successful. For example, it does not appear that spiritual and moral progress has been achieved through the modern pursuit of truth via reason alone. In fact, the failure of modernity to make progress at this vital point, while in possession of technological advances that allow for the obliteration of the human race in a matter of hours, threatens the existence and well-being of all of us.

While it is always risky to attempt to characterize an era while chronologically close to it, many philosophers believe that the modern era has given way to what they call postmodernism. Whereas modernism was predicated upon the assumption that objective truth existed and was discoverable through the right use of human means and reason, postmodernism is built upon very different premises. It takes as its fundamental starting point the assumption that no absolute, objective, and universal truth exists. Instead, truth is always conditioned by the point of view of the knower. Truth is of necessity multiform: I have my truth, you have your truth. In matters intellectual, spiritual, and moral, the postmodern goal is not so much to discover what is true as it is to understand what different people believe about these things. For example, former president Bill Clinton revealed his underlying postmodern assumptions in a speech to Georgetown University. Clinton said, "Nobody's got the truth. You're at a university which basically believes that no one ever has the whole truth, ever . . . We are incapable of ever having the whole truth."[10]

Consider how different that is from the approach of previous generations. Martin Luther launched the Reformation from a university setting by promulgating a series of teachings flowing out of the premise that salvation was by grace alone, through faith alone, in Christ alone. In characteristically modern fashion, his ideas were featured in debates. Luther famously desired to meet leading Roman Catholic theologian John Eck in debate at Leipzig, believing that the pursuit of truth could be advanced by this exchange. A postmodern mindset would not seek to resolve theological differences through debate. Rather, it would celebrate the differences and seek to foster understanding and appreciation between the various parties through interreligious dialogue. Likewise, while many Christian denominations still maintain mission boards and send out missionaries, increasingly the goal is not to convert others as

---

[10] Bill Clinton, speech at Georgetown University, November 7, 2001. Transcript available at: www.georgetown.edu/admin/publicaffairs/protocol_events/events/clinton_glf1 10701.htm. I am indebted to John MacArthur for drawing attention to this citation in his excellent book, *Why One Way? Defending an Exclusive Claim in an Inclusive World* (n.p.[Nashville]; W Publishing Group, 2002), 21.

much as it is to minister to their physical needs and act as a conduit for cultural exchange.

Much of the postmodern agenda sounds compatible with the Christian virtue of forbearance. It is important to realize that postmodernism really is about much more than a heightened view of tolerance. Rather, it is about the nature of truth and how such is ascertained, that is to say, epistemology. In fact, the open-armed tolerance of the postmodern worldview has one glaring exception: it cannot tolerate absolute truth claims of any kind. That places postmodernism squarely at odds with the Bible, which claims to be God-revealed truth in human language, and squarely at odds with Jesus, who claims to be God-revealing truth in human form. Thus, to proclaim the Bible as the truth of God for all men at all times is to be politically incorrect. To proclaim further that this same Bible teaches that salvation is exclusively found in the person and work of Jesus Christ is political incorrectness squared.

So what should Christians do with truth in a postmodern age? I would suggest at least three responses are in order. First, the debates surrounding truth that have emerged in recent years are a reminder of the value of intellectual awareness and apologetics. Ideas have consequences and Christians cannot be willing to cede the world of ideas to unbelievers. Thankfully, Christian apologists have written many critiques of postmodernism. A good number of these represent scholarship of a very deep and profound nature that adequately answer the epistemological challenges of postmodern thought. It does not appear, however, that this apologetic has percolated much into the pulpit, and even less so into the pew.

In most churches, the day has long passed when we can expect to address a congregation of hearers who bring unbridled confidence in the truth of the Bible to church with them. Instead, they have been subjected to a long train of repeated arguments that call into question the veracity of Scripture. The apostle Paul urged Timothy to "do the work of an evangelist." (2 Timothy 4:5, NASB) I do not believe we can do much work along those lines without also doing the work of an apologist, which is one reason we find admonitions like Peter's in the Bible: "But sanctify Christ as Lord in your hearts, always being ready to make a defense to everyone who asks you to give an account for the hope that is in you." (1 Peter 3:15, NASB) In our postmodern climate, one of the first things we are called on to be able to explain is why what we believe about God, Christ, and the Scriptures should have any claim on another person. In other words, we need to be able to defend the premises that Truth exists, has been revealed in the Bible, and we can be understood by the enlightenment of the Holy Spirit.

Second, we need to recommit ourselves to accurate and passionate proclamation of the Bible. As C. H. Spurgeon said, the Bible is like a lion. It does not so much need to be defended as it needs to be turned loose. Then it can fend for itself just fine. Speaking of my own denomination, the Southern Baptist Convention, we talk about our commitment to the Bible an awful lot, but we do not seem to preach it very much. Not surprisingly, nor do our people seem much inclined to live according to its dictates.

I grew up in a traditional Southern Baptist church where biblical exposition from the pulpit ruled the day. The Bible was always the center of any message. On Sunday evenings, our pastor methodically worked his way through the books of the Bible using the technique of verse-by-verse exposition. In any message on any occasion, his hearers could count on the text of a passage being read, interpreted, and applied to the listeners. It mattered but little if the setting was Easter Sunday morning, a funeral, a wedding, or a hayride with wieners over the fire. When I became a pastor myself, I tried to follow this example. Since I had only one pastor all my years growing up, it really was all I could have done. Nobody told me there was another option.

Throughout my ministry, I have been privileged to see numerous people come to join churches where I have served as pastor. More and more over the years, they repeat to me a common message: "Pastor, we so appreciate the fact that you preach the Bible. We are new to the area, and until we visited here, had not been able to find a church that does." Especially in my present pastorate, I have had so many people tell me something similar to this that I decided to try to figure out what exactly is being done in the pulpit of many of our churches. Through the wonders of pod casting and downloadable sermon links at church websites, I have been able to sample a smattering of what passes for preaching in the pulpits of our churches. Thank God for several great exceptions, but I certainly was able to understand why people are saying this to me so frequently. To be honest, I have always felt inadequate as an expositor because I knew I was not in the league of the pastor of my youth. I took some comfort from the fact that most Southern Baptist pastors are not in that league of giants, men like W. A. Criswell, Adrian Rogers, and Bill Bennett. Here is the sobering reality: a pastor who is dead serious about the authority of the Bible and truly makes the Word of God the center of his sermons has already set his church apart from most of them in town. There is no cure for the postmodern demise of truth like the simple, straightforward proclamation of the Bible.

Third, we can respond to the postmodern tide that is steadily eroding truth by remaining stubbornly loyal to Jesus. His plainspoken words are full of power when he rightly claimed to be the embodiment of Truth: "I am the way, and the truth, and the life; no one comes to the Father but through Me." (John 14:6, NASB) We need to learn Christ, imitate Christ, think on Christ, worship Christ, and proclaim Christ. When the apostle Paul saw ungodliness in the church at Ephesus, his advice was a gloss on John 14:6—"But you did not learn Christ in this way, if indeed you have heard Him and have been taught in Him, just as truth is in Jesus." (Ephesians 4:20-21, NASB) Brethren, the truth *is* in Jesus, and *only* in Jesus. Oh, how we need to embrace and cling to Christ! When we do, then we will no doubt be politically incorrect, but we will be rightly related to truth. That should be an easy choice.

3
CAN A PERSON WHO COMMITS SUICIDE GO TO HEAVEN?

The Scriptures are very clear that we are not to take our own lives. The sixth commandment, which tells us, "Thou shalt not kill" (Exodus 20:13), would certainly mean that we are not to kill ourselves. However, I know of nothing in Scripture that identifies suicide as the unforgivable sin.

It is true that, for a person ending his life in the full possession of all his faculties, suicide may represent a final and absolute act of unbelief, a surrender to despair and hopelessness rather than confidence in the living God. In such a case, suicide is the gateway to hell.

But can we ever assume that this is the mental state of everyone who actually commits suicide? My answer is a firm *no* for the following reason. Psychiatrists have studied people who made serious but unsuccessful attempts to take their own lives. When interviewed afterward, 90% of these people said they would not have committed suicide had they waited twenty-four hours. This proves that the act of suicide is often the surrender to an overwhelming but momentary attack of acute depression.

When I think of suicide, my mind goes back to a thirty-five-year-old woman named Jo, who faithfully attended our church. Jo had gone through a devastating divorce. Although she loved her husband dearly, he forsook her for someone else. She counseled with me and with our Minister to Singles. She assured us that she had possessed eternal life since the age of nine, and her lifestyle backed up her testimony. Her parents were faithful members of our church, and her father was a deacon. Then one day to the horror of us all, she committed suicide in her parents' home.

Besides the sheriff and her parents, I was the first person to witness the scene. When I arrived, I found this woman lying in her own blood, with her anguished mother at one end of her body and her grieving father at the other end.

DID JO GO TO HEAVEN OR HELL?

Only God knows whether Jo went to Heaven or hell. But if she did go to hell, that poses a serious theological problem for us. Jesus states in the strongest words that eternal life cannot be lost or taken from anyone (John 10:28-30). The Apostle Paul states that not even death can separate God's child from the "...love of God, which is in Christ Jesus our Lord" (Romans 8:38,39).

When I preached at Jo's funeral, I used Psalm 77:9 as my text: "Has God forgotten to be gracious? Has He in anger shut up His tender mercies?" I answered these questions in my message with an unequivocal *no*. I gave hope to the family that Jo had not forfeited eternal life in her act of suicide but had surrendered to an overwhelming but momentary attack of acute depression that did not represent her true heart and soul.

WHAT DOES THE BIBLE SAY ABOUT SUICIDE?

I certainly don't claim to have the last word on this subject of suicide, but I *have* prayed and studied a great deal about it. I have also talked to one of the leading ethics professor in America about the matter.

The word "suicide" is not once mentioned in the Bible. The Bible itself records only six suicides:

1. King Saul killed himself with his own sword (1 Samuel 31:4).
2. After Saul committed suicide, his armor-bearer did the same, falling on his own sword (1 Samuel 31:4).
3. Ahithophel, who was a counselor to David, killed himself after siding with David's son, Absalom, in an

unsuccessful revolt against the king (2 Samuel 17:23).
4. Zimri, the fifth king of Israel, killed himself after hearing that he had been dethroned (1 Kings 16:18).
5. Samson killed himself while being held captive by the Philistines (Judges 16:30).
6. Judas, the only person recorded in the New Testament who committed suicide, hung himself after betraying Jesus (Matt. 27:5).

In addition to these six instances, Paul prevented the Philippian jailer from committing suicide after all the prisoners were freed by a supernatural earthquake (Acts 16:27,28).

It is very interesting how the Bible deals with these six mentions of people who committed suicide. In each instance, it neither condemns nor condones the suicide. No mention is made of its rightness or wrongness. No lecture on ethics is given. The Scriptures simply record the suicide as a historical act and move on to the next subject.

THE ARGUMENT THAT NONE WHO COMMIT SUICIDE GO TO HEAVEN

Some make a blanket statement that all those who commit suicide must go to hell. Their basis of doing so is the sixth commandment mentioned earlier that tells us, "Thou shalt not kill" (Exodus 20:13). But in the original Hebrew, this verse literally says, "Thou shalt do no murder." This isn't referring to the execution of a criminal by the state. It is talking about an individual who commits the premeditated murder of another individual.

Those who condemn suicide also use First John 3:15, which says, "...No murderer hath eternal life abiding in him." Their argument is that suicide is self-murder and therefore unpardonable. Some have even called it "the unpardonable sin."

But nowhere in the Bible does it say that. There is only one unpardonable sin, and that is blasphemy against the Holy Spirit (*see* Matthew 12). This involves attributing the works of Satan to the Holy Spirit. It has nothing at all to do with suicide.

So on the basis of the sixth commandment, can we definitely say that no suicide can go to Heaven? If we do, we are saying more than the Bible explicitly says. The most we can say is that the Bible may imply this. It is never explicitly stated.

Of course, if a *lost* person commits suicide, that person cannot go to Heaven. If we said he could, we would be teaching the doctrine of a second chance, and Scripture does not teach that. When a lost person dies in *any* manner, including committing suicide, that person cannot go to Heaven. The Bible teaches that no second chance for repentance is available for the lost once they die.

My Conclusions

That leaves me with these observations that I believe are based on scriptural truth:

1. **A saved person in his normal mind will not commit suicide.** Ephesians 5:29 (*KJV*) says, "For no man ever yet hated his own flesh; but nourisheth and cherisheth it, even as the Lord the church." Nothing is so unnatural in the world as suicide. The first law of life is self-preservation, and suicide completely violates that law. This means that a Christian who commits suicide is not in his right mind.

2. **There is great evidence that a few Christians do lose their normal reasoning faculties and, in their confusion, commit suicide.** I have experienced this in my own ministry, as in the case of Jo, the woman I mentioned earlier.

   One more example: A woman once called me and told me that her son, a fine young Christian man, had gotten into a bad marriage. The situation eventually got so bad that her son went over the edge emotionally and mentally and committed suicide. The mother wanted to know what I believed about her son's eternal destination. I told her, "Well, I can tell you this: I am *not* going to say I know that your son went to hell."

3. **Do I preach at the funerals of people who committed suicide? Yes, I certainly do.** Some churches will not even permit the funeral of a suicide. I do not believe that such a policy reflects the Spirit of Jesus. I also don't believe that God has called me to sit in that place of judgment.

As we seek to answer this difficult question, let us consider the fate of King Saul and of Samson, two of the suicides found in Scripture.

1. Was Saul saved? I really doubt this. Before he became the King of Israel, he had shown great evidence of salvation at one point as a young man. But his character was such at the end that I wonder if he was saved. He is not mentioned in Hebrews 11, even though he was the first King of Israel.

2. Samson committed suicide, yet he *is* listed in the list of the faithful (Hebrews 11:32). This would indicate that Heaven was Samson's eternal destination.

So this is my judgment and what I believe: Most suicides involve lost persons who cannot go to Heaven. But there are cases of saved individuals who commit suicide, and these people do go to Heaven.

Someone might say, "Well, if a person who commits suicide can go to Heaven, then *I'm* going to commit suicide, get out of all my troubles, and go on to Heaven!" No, it doesn't work that way. A Christian who commits suicide would not be in his right mind and would thus not be responsible for his actions. But suicide is *not* an option for those who seek a permanent escape route from their difficulties without consequence!

Suicide *is* a great sin. Humanism says that a person's life is his own and that he is free to terminate it at will. That is one of the biggest lies ever propagated. A Christian's life is *not* his own. Taking one's life is an extremely serious matter.

Suicide is taking one's life that was given by God and that only *He* can rightfully take. As Genesis 9:6 (*KJV*) says, "Whoso sheddeth man's blood, by man shall his blood be shed: for in the image of God made he man." Certainly this verse would speak against suicide as well as the murder of another human being.

But in every situation, we must always leave room for God's infinite grace and mercy. Certainly we cannot know the last thoughts that go through a person's mind before he or she dies. Consider the case of someone who decides to end his life and jumps off a thirty-story building. If that person changes his mind on his way to the ground and thinks, *This was a mistake. God forgive me! I shouldn't have done this!* isn't there room in God's grace for that person's repentance from his final sin?

4
HELL- A STATE OF MIND OR A REAL ESTATE?

A recent book bears the arresting title Hell Under Fire. This title describes succinctly the growing attitude of many toward hell. Since the Enlightenment of the 18th Century, hell has been under attack by the intellectually elite and secularists, but during the last fifty years, attacks on the historic doctrine of hell have come from within the church itself. "In a recent survey, it was determined that 35% of Baptists; 54% of Presbyterians, 58% of Methodists, and 60% of Episcopalians DO NOT Believe in a literal place called HELL! 71% of the 8 leading seminaries in the United States Do Not Believe in either Heaven or Hell."[11]

Two doctrines have been advanced by some evangelicals who claim the support of Scripture, but which in fact deny the existence of the place of torment which the Bible calls Hell:

(1) **Universalism** – the view that in the end all persons will experience the love of God and eternal life. This heresy goes back to Origen in the second century but has been rejected by the historic church as plain heresy through the ages.
(2) **Annihilationism** – the view that the wicked will be ultimately exterminated and cease to exist. The Jehovah Witnesses and the 7th Day Adventist church teach this error. Dr. J. W. Stott and Dr. Clark Pinnock, once highly respected in evangelical circles, espouse this viewpoint.[12]

Another approach intended to make hell more palapable has been to seek to diminish the horrors of hell by human rationalizations or unbiblical misconceptions:

---

[11] Steven Cook, "The Saddest Thing About Going to Hell," www.sermoncentral.com, October 18, 2000, p. 1.
[12] Editors, Morgan and Peterson, Hell Under Fire, Grand Rapids, Michigan: Zondervan, 2004, pp. 30, 31, 213,27.

Misconception # 1 – Hell is only a "State of Mind," not a "Real Estate" as Scripture says.

Misconception # 2 – Hell is a "State of Nothingness." The Anglican Church has officially adopted this viewpoint. "It is our conviction that the reality of hell (and indeed of heaven) is the ultimate affirmation of the reality of human freedom. Hell is not eternal torment, but it is the final and irrevocable choosing of that which is opposed to God so completely and so absolutely that the only end is total non-being."[13]

Misconception # 3 – "After I spend a time in hell, I'll be able to get out."

Misconception # 4 – "There will be a second chance to repent after death."

Misconception # 5 – "Hell won't be bad, for I'll be there with my buddies."

Misconception # 6 – "My God would never send anyone to hell." I was witnessing to a lady once who made this very statement to me, to which I surprised her by replying, "Right, your God would never send anyone to hell, but there is something radically wrong with your God: He is not the God of the Bible. He does not exist."

Misconception # 7 – Hell is a "state of mind" rather than "real estate."

All of these misconceptions are clearly blown apart (shot down) by Jesus in Luke 16:19-31, when He tells of a definite rich man who after death went to Hades and "And being in torments in Hades, he lifted up his eyes and saw Abraham afar off, and Lazarus in his bosom.

---

[13] Quoted in <u>Hell Under Fire</u>, p. 33.

"Then he cried and said, 'Father Abraham, have mercy on me, and send Lazarus that he may dip the tip of his finger in water and cool my tongue; for I am tormented in this flame.'"(verses 23-24). Jesus clearly said the rich man was suffering the torments of hell from which there was no escape and no "buddies" to give him comfort. From the story, one concludes that the rich man was in solitary isolation.

For the grossly ungodly and rebellious, hell is a joke. For example, one person said to another, "If in heaven, we don't meet, hand in hand, we'll beat the heat, and if it ever gets too hot, Pepsi Cola hits the spot." Mark Twain said, "I'll take heaven for the climate, but hell for the society" (company). Ted Turner remarked, "I'm looking forward to dying and going to hell because I know that is where I am headed." Even the religious poke fun at hell. One of my liberal professors in seminary made this observation one day in class, "I am not interested in the furniture in heaven, nor the temperature of hell."

The story is told that a Baptist, Methodist and Charismatic went to hell. All were surprised they had ended up in such a place. The Baptist said, "It's strange I'm here because I got saved and was told if once saved I would always be saved, yet I end up here." The Methodist said, "My church taught me there was no hell, and yet I find myself in hell." The Charismatic, being an incurable optimist, after hearing his Baptist and Methodist brothers complain, burst forth with these words, "You know what I am going to do: I'm not going to worry a moment about being in hell. In fact I am going to confess that I am not even here."

I myself became a part of a ridiculous story about hell told by some of my church members who knew something of my excessive zeal in raising money for missions. The story went like this: "Billy Graham and Bill Bennett went to hell and when they met each other they devised a plan to empty hell. Billy said he would preach and get everybody saved and Bill

Bennett said he would raise enough money to air-condition the place."

I have shared all of the above to show how stupid, wicked, and ridiculous have been man's attempts to repudiate the doctrine of hell. C. S. Lewis was told about a gravestone inscription that read, "Here lies an atheist – all dressed up and no where to go." Lewis quietly replied, "I bet he wishes that were so."

Where, then, do we go to find the truth, the whole truth, and nothing but the truth about hell. We dare not trust the theories of men, but how can we rule them out? Seven hundred years ago, Thomas A'Kempis, gave us the answer in these memorable words, "The voice of the divine rules out a multitude of human opinions." Thus if we would have the final and ultimate truth about hell, we must go to God's written (infallible) word, the Holy Bible, and "Let the Bible speak." When we go to the Word, written and living, we will find that hell is an unending state of punishment and exclusion from the presence of the Lord.

Since by common consent Jesus Christ, the Son of God, is the central authority for Christians, His teachings on hell are a "primary point of reference in assessing the propriety of what the church has most commonly affirmed."[14] "Jesus' teaching on hell is found primarily in the Gospels. But in a sense the whole of New Testament teaching on hell can be viewed as coming from Jesus, since writers like Paul, Peter, and John, claim to be passing along what He taught about hell (Romans 15:19, 30; 1 Cor. 2:10-14; 7:40; Ephesians 3:5; 1 Thess. 1:5; 1 Timothy 4:1)."[15] "The book of Hebrews and Revelation actually amplify aspects of Jesus' teaching on hell."[16]

---

[14] Ibid, Hell Under Fire, p. 68.
[15] Ibid. p. 77
[16] Ibid. p. 77

What, then, shall we believe and preach about hell? There are six stupendous facts we need to affirm:

1. **Hell is real** – Matthew 5:22, 29-30; 7:13; 8:10-12; 10:26-28; 13:40-42; 47-50; 18:8-9' 23:33; 25:41, 45-46.
2. "**Hell is vividly described** on the pages of the New Testament."[17]
3. **Metaphors are used to describe hell**. "We are not under constraint to resolve how utter darkness can also have perpetually burning flames. These...are metaphors."[18] "Here is a vital point – metaphors are used precisely in order to describe realities greater than themselves. Hell itself is not metaphorical but real; these vivid metaphors point to a reality more awful than prosaic language is required."[19]
4. "**Hell, though prepared for the devil and his angels (demons), is shared by real human beings**...Hell is the wasteland of humanity, inhabited by all those who reject Christ and His revelation."[20]
5. **Hell is eternal if heaven is eternal.** Jesus categorically states in Matthew 25:46, "And these (the lost without Christ) will go away into eternal punishment, but the righteous into eternal life." Some hold that "eternal means 'unending in conscious experience' when referring to heaven, but 'unending only in effect' when referring to hell – that is, the unbelieving are destroyed and then cease existence. This view has a pedigree extending back several centuries. In response to this position, for now we may simply cite the results of North America's earliest Bible scholar, Moses Stuart, who already in 1830 carefully examined the biblical data in the ancient languages and arrived at this conclusion:

---

[17] Ibid. p. 226
[18] Ibid. p. 226
[19] Ibid. p. 227
[20] Ibid. p. 227

The result seems to be plain, and philologically and exegetically certain. It is this; either the declarations of the Scriptures do not establish the facts, that God and His glory and praise and happiness are endless; nor that the happiness of the righteous in a future world, is endless; or else they establish the fact, that the punishment of the wicked is endless. The whole stand or fall together. There can, in the very nature of antithesis, be no room for rational doubt here, in what manner we should interpret the declarations of the sacred writers, WE MUST EITHER ADMIT THE ENDLESS MISERY OF HELL, OR GIVE UP THE ENDLESS HAPPINESS OF HEAVEN."[21]

6. **There is One Way of Salvation out of hell** – John 3:36; Acts 4:12; John 14:6; 2 Timothy 2:5; 1 Cor. 3:11.

The biblical truth about hell should be preached from every pulpit in the land. For homiletical purpose, I suggest the following simple, alliterative outline:

1. **Hell is Literal in its Existence**. Jesus spoke much, much more about hell than He spoke about heaven. Jesus warned, "If thy right eye offend thee, pluck it out; for it is better to go with one eye in this life than to go to hell" – Matthew 5:29. Again Jesus said, "Whosoever shall say thou fool, shall be in danger of hell fire" – Matthew 5:22. Do you think Jesus would have told us to do whatever it takes to stay out of a place that did not exist?

---

[21] Ibid. pp. 75-76

2. **Hell is Lethal (deadly) in its Punishment**.
"The Bible depicts the horrors of hell in many different ways:
   A. A place of darkness.
      1. Peter says it is chains of darkness – 2 Peter 2:4.
      2. Jude also says it is chains of darkness – Jude: 6.
      3. Jesus says it is a place of outer darkness – Matthew

   B. A place of constant fatigue. In Revelation 14:11, the Bible says the smoke of their torment ascendeth up forever and ever and there is no rest. How would you like to come home from work and never get any rest?
   C. Hell is also a bottomless pit – Revelation 20:3.
   D. Hell is also a place of writhing worms. Mark 9:38 says, "Where the worm dieth not." Jesus pointed to the Valley of Hinnom (the garbage waste dump for Jerusalem) and said that's what Hell is going to be like. Job says that man is a worm – Job 2:36. Worm describes the depraved nature of man. We used to sing, "Would He devote that sacred head for such a worm as I." That is why folks don't get saved, they think they are as good as God. They think they are as smart as God. We refuse to admit that we are as worms in the sight of God.
   E. Hell is a place of vivid memory. Abraham said to the rich man, "Remember." People in hell have real bodies. Luke 16:19-28 tells of:
      1. eyes – verse 23

2. tongue – verse 24
3. mouth – verse 24
4. mind – verse 25
5. ears – verse 25 (He could hear)

The inhabitants of hell will remember the times that they could have been saved and they will remember those who said nothing to them about being saved.

F. <u>Hell is also a place of gnashing of teeth.</u> There are only 2 reasons why someone gnashes teeth: pain and anger.
G. <u>Hell is a place of weeping and wailing.</u>
H. <u>Hell is a place of real, literal fire (or something worse).</u> [22]

3. **Hell is Lasting in Duration**. As already stated above, the teachings of Annihilationism seeks to deny the eternality of hell on Scriptural grounds, but this is clearly refuted in Matthew 25:46 and many other passages. "And these will go away into everlasting punishment, but the righteous into eternal life."

4. **Hell is Lovingly Escapable**. The saddest thing about going to hell will be to realize that you do not have to go there. "For God so loved the world, that whosoever (write your name there) believeth in Him, shall not perish but have eternal life" (John 3:16). "...It is not the will of your Father in heaven that any one should perish (go to hell) but all come to repentance" (2 Peter 3:9).

I read that Calvin Coolidge was presiding over the US Senate when one Senator said to another Senator, "You go to hell." The latter was greatly perturbed and cried out to Coolidge to condemn the accuser. Then

---

[22] Ronnie Thrower, "The Reality of Hell," sermoncentral.com, March 13, 2002, pp. 2-3

Coolidge replied, "I have just read the rules, Senator, and they say you do not have to go to hell." In my own experience as a pastor, a member of my flock came to my office one day, complaining that another brother had told him to go to hell. I said to that person, "I have good news for you. You don't have to go there."

If you go to hell, it will be because you have rejected God's pardon by not admitting you are a lost sinner, repenting, and trusting Jesus as your Lord and Savior.

No man in his right mind on death row is going to turn down a pardon, to escape death.

> A preacher was invited to address the inmates of a large penitentiary. The afternoon before he was to speak he paid a visit to the institution. The warden showed him around, and at last they came to the chapel. It was a large auditorium seating about fifteen hundred people. "It will be full tomorrow morning, sir," said the officer. It was not the number of seats, but rather the two particular seats on the front row that intrigued the preacher. "Why are those two chairs here in front draped in black?" he asked. The warden replied, "The two men who will occupy those seats tomorrow are under sentence of death. On Monday they go to the electric chair!" "Under sentence of death," repeated the minister quietly. And then he said, "Do I understand that this will be the last service they will ever attend?" "Yes, sir," was the reply. "Your sermon will be the last one they will ever hear."
>
> The preacher had seen all he wanted to see. He must find a place to be alone and do some quiet thinking. When he reached home, he

went to his study, took out the sermon he had prepared, reviewed it, then tore it up! "This is no use," he said. "It does not meet the need." Then falling on his knees, he prayed, "O God, give me a message for those two men who will be sitting in those draped chairs."[23]

There are draped chairs in every congregation. Therefore, the preacher must preach the reality of an eternal hell but also the reality of God's pardon that no one go there. Three naughty boys removed the Stop Sign at a dangerous intersection, and three people were killed. Those boys were convicted of second-degree murder. Brother Pastor, have you removed the "Warning Sign" against hell in your preaching? If so, you are guilty of murdering souls in hell and it's high time you begin to preach what God, not man, says about hell.

I believe the most disconcerting aspect of the modern evangelical attack on hell has been the denial of its existence by some of the most important leaders of the 20th century: Stott[24], Pinnock[25], Bruce[26] and Pope Paul II.[27]

On the other hand many fine evangelical scholars have brilliantly defended the doctrine of the existence of a burning hell as taught in Scripture and held by the church for 2000 years such as R. Albert Mohler, Jr., Gregory K. Beale, Daniel I. Block, Sinclair B Ferguson, Douglas J. Moo, Christopher W. Morgan, J. I. Packer, Robert A. Peterson, and Robert W. Yar-

---

[23] Quoted in, Bill Bennett, <u>Thirty Minutes to Raise the Dead</u>, Nashville, Tennessee: Thomas Nelson, 1991, pp. 146-147.
[24] Ed. Morgan and Peterson, <u>Hell Under Fire</u>, Grand Rapids, Michigan: Zondervan, 2004, p. 30
[25] Ibid. p. 213
[26] Ibid. p. 31
[27] Ibid. p. 27

brough, Adrian Rogers, Paige Patterson, Daniel Akin, R. G. Lee, and James Kennedy.

Albert Mohler writes, "The temptation to revise the doctrine of hell – to remove the sting and scandal of everlasting conscious punishment – is understandable. But it's also a major test of evangelical conviction. This is no theological trifle. As one observer has asked, "Could it be that the only result of attempts, however, well meaning, to air-condition hell, is to ensure that more and more people wind up there.

Hell demands our attention in the present, and now confronts evangelicals with a critical test of theological and biblical integrity. Hell may be denied, but it will not disappear."[28]

A biblical preacher was reproached by one of his hearers after he preached a strong sermon on hell with these words, "Pastor, don't you realize that the more up-to-date pastors have quit preaching on hell?" To which the pastor replied, "Yes, I know that, but the problem is they have not done away with it." My plea to all who read this chapter on hell: Don't go there!

---

[28] Ibid, Hell Under Fire, p. 41.

5
Same-Sex Marriage

An all-out effort to destroy the institution of marriage has been going on now for a generation. Those behind this concerted effort are finally within reach of their goal as they focus on the issue of *same-sex marriage*.

No event in our time is as far-reaching in its potentially disastrous consequences as this movement to legitimize same-sex marriages. Why is this? Because the destruction of marriage will mean the destruction of everything we hold dear the family, children, common decency, religious liberty, even civilization itself.

There have been at least seven major steps in the campaign to destroy the institution of marriage:

1. **The Sexual Revolution:** "Make love, not war!" shouted the students in the sixties. This mindset made a joke of marriage. Sexually transmitted diseases, including the onset of HIV/Aids epidemic, has reached epidemic proportions.

2. **No-Fault Divorce:** The world's first no-fault divorce law was signed into law in California in 1969. This would prove to be an extremely damaging blow to marriage. Suddenly it was easier for a spouse to legally terminate his or her marriage than to break a pool maintenance contract.

3. **The Normalization of Cohabitation:** Cohabitation was once referred to as "living in sin," but its rate of occurrence has increased 850% since 1960.

4. **Granting a Marriage License for Homosexual Marriage:** On November 18, 2003, Massachusetts' highest court ruled that preventing same-sex couples from marrying is not permissible under the State Constitution. Following this ruling, Massachusetts

began issuing marriage license to homosexuals on May 17, 2004.

5. **The Killing of Babies in Mothers' Wombs:** Murder was legalized with the 1973 Roe vs. Wade Supreme Court decision, resulting in the death of forty-five million babies   a horrific number that grows daily.

6. **The Legalization of Sodomy:** Alas! On June 26, 2003, the Supreme Court ruled that the U.S. Constitution guarantees a right to sodomy. This case is now known as the infamous *Lawrence vs. Texas* decision.

7. **The Action of the U.S. Senate:** On July 13, 2004, the U.S. Senate voted down an amendment to the Constitution defining marriage as between one man and one woman. Forty-eight senators voted for the amendment; sixty were required for its passage.

THE CONSEQUENCES OF SAME-SEX MARRIAGE

1. Same-sex marriage *defies* the definition of marriage given by God the Father in the Garden of Eden.

> This divine plan was revealed to Adam and Eve in the Garden of Eden and then described succinctly in Genesis 2:24, where we read, *"Therefore shall a man leave his father and his mother, and shall cleave unto his wife: and they shall be one flesh"* (KJV). With those twenty-two words, God announced the ordination of the family, long before He established the

two other great human institutions, the church and the government.[29]

2. Same-sex marriage *disregards* the teaching of Jesus on marriage. When asked about divorce, Jesus reiterated the very words of God the Father:

> **The Pharisees also came to Him, testing Him, and saying to Him, "Is it lawful for a man to divorce his wife for just any reason?"**
>
> **And He answered and said to them, "Have you not read that He who made them at the beginning 'made them male and female.'"**
>
> **And said, 'For this reason a man shall leave his father and mother and be joined to his wife, and the two shall become one flesh'?**
>
> **So then, they are no longer two but one flesh. Therefore what God has joined together, let not man separate."**

Matthew 19:3-6

3. Same-sex marriage *discounts* the teaching of the Apostle Paul. Paul held the same view of marriage as did God the Father and Jesus the Son:

> **"For this reason a man shall leave his father and mother and be joined to his wife, and the two shall become one flesh."**

Ephesians 5:31

---

[29] James Dobson, *Marriage Under Fire* (Sisters, OR: Multnomah Publishers, 2004), p. 7.

4. Same-sex marriage *denies* the teaching of the historic church Protestant, Orthodox, and Catholic for 2,000 years. No legitimate Christian body, except the Episcopal Church, has ever endorsed same-sex marriage.

5. Same-sex marriage *disregards* the fact that no civilization, no matter how corrupt, has practiced same-sex marriage. Only two countries, the Netherlands and Belgium, have actually legalized "gay marriage," and only in recent years.

> The institution of marriage in those countries is rapidly dying, with most young couples cohabiting or choosing to remain single. In some areas of Norway, 80 percent of first-born children are conceived out of wedlock, as are 60 percent of subsequent births. It appears that tampering with the ancient plan for males and females spells doom for the family and for everything related to it.[30]

6. Same-sex marriage *deprives* males and females of that intimate relationship ordained by a loving God, which is essential to their well being physical, emotional and spiritual.

> One reason the preservation of the family is critical to the health of nations is the enormous influence the sexes have on each other. They are specifically designed to "fit" together, both physically and emotionally, and neither is entirely comfortable without the other.[31]

---

[30] Ibid., p. 9.
[31] Ibid., p. 10.

7. Same-sex marriage *develops* an environment in which every form of sexual behavior will flourish. "The introduction of legalized gay marriages will lead inexorably to polygamy and other alternatives to one-man/one-woman unions. In Utah, polygamist Tom Green, who claims five wives, is citing <u>Lawrence vs. Texas</u> as the legal authority for his appeal."[32]

Moreover, "public schools in every state will embrace homosexuality. Adoption laws will be instantly obsolete. Foster-care programs will be impacted dramatically."[33]

8. Same-sex marriage will *devastate* children.

> The implications for children in a world of decaying families are profound. Because homosexuals are rarely monogamous, often having as many as three hundred or more partners in a lifetime some studies say it is typically more than one thousand children in those polyamorous situations are caught in a perpetual coming and going. It is devastating to kids, who by their nature are enormously conservative creatures. They like things to stay just the way they are, and they hate change.[34]

9. Same-sex marriage will *deprive* us of our religious liberty.

> In order to get a perspective on where the homosexual activist movement is taking us, one can sim-

---

[32] Ibid., p. 48.
[33] Ibid., pp. 56-57.
[34] Ibid., pp. 53-54.

ply look at our neighbors to the north. Canada is leading the way on this revolutionary path. I could cite dozens of examples indicating that religious freedom in that country is dying. Indeed, on April 28, 2004, the Parliament passed Bill C-250, which effectively criminalized speech or writings that criticize homosexuality. Anything deemed to be "homophobic" is punishable by six months in prison or other severe penalties.

Pastors and priests in Canada are wondering if they can preach from Leviticus or Romans 1 or other passages from the writings of the apostle Paul. Will a new Bible be mandated that is bereft of "hate speech"? Consider this: A man who owned a printing press in Canada was fined over $40,000 for refusing to print stationery for a homosexual activist organization.[35]

10. Same-sex marriage *demands* the judgment of God upon our nation. Listen to Paul's ominous warning in Romans 1:

> **Because of this, God gave them over to shameful lusts. Even their women exchanged natural relations for unnatural ones.**
> **In the same way the men also abandoned natural relations with women and were inflamed with lust for one another. Men committed indecent acts with other men, and received in themselves the due penalty for their perversion.**

---

[35] Ibid., pp. 59-60.

> **Furthermore, since they did not think it worthwhile to retain the knowledge of God, he gave them over to a depraved mind, to do what ought not to be done.**
> **Romans 1:26-28 *NIV***

In this chapter, Paul sets forth the steps that lead to a nation's destruction. One of the final steps is the acceptance of the homosexual lifestyle, including same-sex marriage.

How Can We Prevent This Final Step?

Renowned Christian psychologist and author James Dobson recommends seven steps that you as a Christian citizen can take to help bring about a godly conclusion to this all-out attack on marriage. I will add the eighth step:

1. Contact your senators and representatives in Washington. Write a letter or place a phone call. I hear repeatedly that our leaders are not receiving public feedback regarding the Federal Marriage Amendment.

2. Register to vote. Do it now in order to ensure that your voice will be heard during the next election.

3. Take part in radio and television call-in programs that discuss the subject.

4. Volunteer to teach a class or hold a seminar in your church, synagogue, or community to educate others about family-related issues.

5. Put up lawn signs and distribute bumper stickers proclaiming the sanctity of marriage.

6. Organize a debate in your community on this issue.

7. Familiarize yourself with the realities of judicial tyranny. A good website to check out would be www.stopjudicialtyranny.com.

8. *Pray* earnestly that God's truth and His will would prevail in this matter of same-sex marriage. Second Chronicles 7:14 gives us the divine pattern:

> **If my people, which are called by my name, shall humble themselves, and pray, and seek my face, and turn from their wicked ways; then will I hear from heaven, and will forgive their sin, and will heal their land.**

God has called us to be the salt of the earth and the voice of righteousness on this earth. If we stay silent, we will have no one to blame but ourselves for the ground that is lost to the enemy. The future of marriage, of the family, and of civilization itself is at stake and as Christians, we have the ability by God's grace to make the difference.

6
ABORTION:
LET SCRIPTURE AND SCIENCE SPEAK

In order to deal adequately with the abortion issue, we first need to answer sixteen pertinent questions.

1. **What is abortion?** The *New World Dictionary* gives this definition of "abortion": "The expulsion of the fetus from the womb before it is sufficiently developed to survive."[36] The word "fetus" is Latin for *progeny, descendant,* or *young one.*

2. **Is abortion a big problem in the modern world?** Let the following facts speak for themselves.

3. **Why are children aborted?** The Alan Guttmacher Institute, which is the research arm of Planned Parenthood, states:

   - 1% of mothers who abort are victims of incest or rape.
   - 1% had fetal abnormalities.
   - 4% had a doctor who said their health would worsen if they continued the pregnancy.
   - 50% said that they didn't want to be a single parent or that they had problems in their current relationships.
   - 66% stated that they could not afford a child.
   - 75% said that the child would interfere with their lives.[37]
   - **Conclusion:** 95% of children are killed for reasons of convenience, *not* for reasons of incest, rape, an abnormal condition of the unborn, or the health of the mother.

---

[36] David B. Gurlnik, ed., *Webster's New World Dictionary of the American Language* (New York: World Publishers, 1972), p. 4.
[37] Charles R. Swindoll, *Sanctity of Life* (Dallas: Word Publishing, 1990), p. 12.

4. **When are children aborted?**

    - 50% of all abortions are performed at 8 weeks.
    - 25% are performed at 9 to 10 weeks.
    - 14% are performed at 11 to 12 weeks.
    - 5% are performed at 13 to 15 weeks.
    - 4% are performed at 16 to 20 weeks.
    - 2% are performed after 20 weeks.[38]

5. **How many children are aborted?** "Worldwide, 55 million unborn children are killed every year. If you are like me, you can't wrap your mind around that large of a number. To help us to do so, let me break down the number into days, hours, and minutes:

    - Around the world, 150,685 children are killed by abortion every day.
    - Every hour, 6,278 children are killed by abortion.
    - Every minute, 105 children are killed by abortion.

    Those are the reported cases. If you are an American citizen, no doubt your greatest interest is in the number of abortions in your own nation. Let me break down that number using a national statistic:

    - 1,600,000 babies are aborted in the United States every year.
    - That means 4,383 babies are aborted every day.
    - 183 babies are aborted per hour.
    - 3 babies are aborted per minute."[39]

    That's correct 3 children are killed every minute in the United States!

---

[38] Ibid., pp. 12-13.
[39] Ibid., p. 13.

6. **How do war deaths compare with our abortion deaths?**

Revolutionary War	25,324
Civil War	498,332
World War I	116,708
World War II	407,316
Korean War	54,246
Vietnam War	58,655
Gulf War	128[40]
Iraqi War	4,178+[41]
Total	**1,164,887**

War on the Unborn
(since abortion was legalized in 1973 to 2008)

Fifty million is more than the populations of some nations! Not only are the spiritual and emotional consequences staggering, but consider the economic loss. Suppose we had these fifty million persons paying into Social Security! Would not that amount have saved the Social Security trust fund from imminent bankruptcy? In a word, abortion is equivalent to genocide.

7. **Does abortion reduce child abuse, as its proponents have said?** Exactly the opposite has taken place. There has been between a 500 and 600% increase in child abuse since *Roe vs. Wade* (1973). This can be directly attributed to the natural progression of a wrong conclusion, i.e., *if I have the right to kill my child before he or she is born, I have the right of life and death over my child after he or she is born.* The logic is irrefutable. This leads me to say that abortion cheapens life and paves the way for its destruction up and down the line.

---

[40] Ibid. p. 14.

8. **Does capital punishment violate the sanctity of life?** It does just the opposite. Genesis 9:6 (*NIV*) reads, "Whoever sheds the blood of man, by man shall his blood be shed; for in the image of God has God made man." This passage is a divine mandate for capital punishment in the case of murder. The moral basis for capital punishment is the sanctity of life. The biblical ethic is that because humankind is endowed with the image of God, a person's life is so sacred that any malicious destruction of that life must be punished by execution (*see* Exodus 20:13 and 21:12).

9. **When does life begin?** If life does not begin until after birth, abortion is but the removal of physical tissue, a minor operation. "An abortion operation can be done during lunchtime," observed one pro-abortionist. However, if life begins *before* birth, abortion is the destruction of that life, which translates into murder.

   This is not to charge all abortionists with outright first-degree murder. R.C. Sproul observes:

   > Given the understanding of the term murder (premeditated killing of a person), we must be careful to insist that pro-abortionists and pro-choice proponents are not advocating murder. They are not endorsing the premeditated, with malice aforethought, willful destruction of human persons. Almost universally, the proponents of abortion act on the conviction that what is being aborted is less than a living human being. To state premeditated intent

is absent is not to say that it is legitimate.[42]

It is very sad that most of our citizens do not know what the Bible says on the origin of life. This is due to the failure of the Church. Although science cannot agree on this question, the Holy Scripture clearly teaches that life begins at conception and even before.

Let the Scriptures speak for themselves.

A. Genesis 1:27: "So God created man in his own image...."
Only human life by God's design possesses His image. No plant or animal holds that distinction.
B. Exodus 20:13 (*NIV*): "You shall not murder."
Why not? Because life is so precious and unique that the Creator Himself commands that it be protected and preserved.
C. Genesis 4:1 (*KJV*): "And Adam knew Eve his wife; and she conceived [Cain] and bare Cain, and said, I have gotten a man from the Lord."
Notice that Eve conceived Cain, and it was Cain she also bore. Cain was in the picture from conception.
D. Genesis 25:22: "And the children [Jacob and Esau] struggled together within her...."
The Lord went on to tell Rebecca, the mother, that two nations were in her womb. Do you think God regarded Jacob and Esau as "blobs of protoplasm" and "non-personalities"?
E. Job 3:3: "Let the day perish wherein I was born, and the night in which it was said, there is a man child conceived."
"Man child means *boy* in our language. Job believed that he was a boy at conception.

---

[42] R. C. Sproul, *Abortion: A Rational Look at an Emotional Issue* (Colorado Springs: NavPress, 1990).

F. Jeremiah 1:5 (*NIV*): "Before I formed you in the womb I knew you, before you were born I set you apart; I appointed you as a prophet to the nations."

God tells Jeremiah that He knew him and called him to preach before he was born. *Personal note:* My mother told me that she dedicated me to the Lord as His servant when I was in her womb. A similar passage is found in Isaiah 49:1-5.

G. Psalm 51:5 (*NIV*): "Surely I was sinful at birth, sinful from the time my mother conceived me."

David is saying that not only his biological substance, but also his moral disposition, dated back to conception.

H. Luke 1:40-44: "Where she [Mary] entered Zechariah's home and greeted Elizabeth. When Elizabeth heard Mary's greeting, the baby leaped in her womb, and Elizabeth was filled with the Holy Spirit. In a loud voice she exclaimed: 'Blessed are you among women, and blessed is the child you will bear! But why am I so favored, that the mother of my Lord should come to me? As soon as the sound of your greeting reached my ears, the baby in my womb leaped for joy.'"

These verses show that before John was born, he exhibited cognition and emotion. As a baby in his mother's womb, he leaped for joy, and his joy was prompted by the recognition of the presence of the unborn Messiah. Are we to regard both John and Jesus as fetal tissue, or as real persons?

I. Psalm 139:13-16 (*KJV*): "For thou hast possessed my reins: thou hast covered me in my mother's womb. I will praise thee; for I am fearfully and wonderfully made: marvelous are thy works; and that my soul knoweth right well. My substance was not hid from thee, when I was made in secret, and curiously wrought in the lowest parts of the earth. Thine eyes did see my substance, yet being unperfect; and in thy book all my members were written, which in continuance were fashioned, when as yet there was none of them."

- The phrase "possess my reins" (literally "possess my kidneys") means that God formed all the internal organs of David.
- "Covered me" in verse 13 literally means "knitted me together."
- "My substance " literally "my bones" refers to the skeletal frame.
- "Made in secret" is equivalent to "made in the womb."
- "Curiously wrought" literally means "embroidered."
- "In the lowest parts of the earth" is simply Hebraic poetic language for the formation of the child in the darkness of the womb.
- "My substance yet being unperfect" in verse 16 refers to the embryo.

This verse affirms God's prior knowledge of David's life all the way from the pre-embryonic state to the end of his life and into eternity.

10. **Do the arguments for abortion justify its practice?**

   A. **Argument #1:** *The unborn fetus is not a person.*
   In Roe vs. Wade, the Supreme Court ruled that the unborn fetus is not a person as defined by our Constitution and therefore has no rights as a person. The Bible shows otherwise.
   B. **Argument #2:** *The woman has control of her own body.*
   The Supreme Court ruled that this right was implied by the right-to-privacy provisions in the Constitution. But the right to life transcends the right to privacy. No persons, including women, have an absolute right to do anything they wish

with their bodies. The fetus, although connected to a woman and sharing geographical space within her body, has a distinct genetic imprint and is in essence a separate entity, *not* a part of the woman's body. The father, grandparents, and other ancestors contribute to the unique genetic structure of the fetus. Is the woman free to destroy her body through suicide? To mutilate it? To use it as a battering ram to injure others?

C. **Argument #3:** *Abortion is a necessary form of birth control, preventing the overpopulation of the world.*
Yes, birth control is justified, but not by abortion. Birth control is the prevention of life before it occurs. Abortion is the destruction of life *after* it has occurred.

D. **Argument #4:** *A woman should not give birth to a life she does not want.*
A woman may have a vote on this before conception, but not after. All life is given by God, and it can only be taken by God (Job 1:21).

E. **Argument #5:** *No woman should have to bear a child fathered by a criminal.*
Less than 1% of abortions are because of rape. Abortion would be a non-issue if it occurred only in the case of rape.

F. **Argument #6:** *Psychologically, it is unwise for a woman to have a baby she does not want.*
As a pastor, I have found that women who have experienced abortion often undergo indescribable psychological problems. Says Bill Hybels, a great pastor of thousands in Chicago, "I have talked to many women who say to me, "Please tell the truth to the women of the church. Abortion is not a quick fix. What accompanies the quick fix may-

very well be a lifetime of regret shadows, sinister thoughts, crippling dreams, and nightmares.'"[43]

G. **Argument # 7:** *Poor, ignorant women will get back-alley abortions and die.*
This is a concern to me, especially in the case of ignorant, victimized women. But the answer is not to legalize abortion, no more than it would be to legalize terrorism so terrorists would stop making homemade bombs and destroying themselves.

11. **Should the government be involved in the abortion question?** Government is a divine gift. Its role is to restrain evil so that human beings can live in peace and safety. According to Scripture, the authority and power of the state rests in the authority and power of God (*see* Romans 13). The protection of human life is at the head of proper governmental concern. Both the Declaration of Independence and the United States Constitution say as much. Jefferson wrote, "The care of human life and not its destruction...is the first and only legitimate object of good government."[44]

12. **Should the Church speak out on the abortion issue?** The First Amendment forbids the government to establish a religion. When the Church calls on the state to prohibit abortion, the state is not being asked to establish a religion, nor is the state being asked to be the Church. *The Church is merely asking the state to be the state.* If it is the role of the state to protect, sustain, and maintain human life, and if it is the conviction of the Church that abortion involves the destruction of human life, then it follows that the Church has the right to call on the state to outlaw abortion. This is *not* a violation of the separation of church and state.

---

[43] Bill Hybels, *One Church's Answer to Abortion* (Chicago, Illinois: Moody Press, 1986), p. 16.
[44] Thomas Jefferson to Maryland Republicans, 1809, ME 16:359.

13. **What if you are not sure?** The New Testament teaches that conscience must not be violated in making ethical choices (Romans 14:23). Here is good advice when making any ethical choice, but in particular when making a decision about abortion: *"When in doubt, don't."*

14. **Is abortion the unpardonable sin?** Although what one has done cannot be undone, a person can be forgiven. Forgiveness is one of the marvels of God's grace. Its healing power is magnificent. For those who have been involved in abortion, God does not require that they spend the rest of their lives walking around with a big red "A" on their chests. He *does* require, however, that they repent of their sin and come to Him for the cleansing of forgiveness. When God forgives His children, they are forgiven. When God cleanses His children, they are made clean. This is cause for great celebration!

15. **What should be your response?** If you care about the slaughter of the innocent, then for God's sake, speak up! Speak to your family. Speak to your neighbor. Speak to your friend. Speak to your doctor. Speak to your minister. Speak to your congressman. Let your voice be heard in a chorus of protest. Yours is only one voice, *but it is a voice*. Use it!

> In my treatment of abortion, I have for the most part treated it from a theological and philosophical standpoint. However, I think it would be appropriate to look at it from a scientific perspective; therefore, I am sharing below an address given by my granddaughter, Miss Angela Bennett, who is now an honor student – science major at Hendricks College, Conway, Arkansas. She is also planning to earn her PhD in science. Her address which follows won first place in an Arkansas State-wide competition.

- **Abortion from a Scientific Prospective by Angela Bennett, Dr. Bill Bennett's granddaughter:**

The sea turtle is an animal that appears on the endangered species list. In America, if you damage or destroy a sea turtle egg, you can be fined or put in jail. What is wrong with the fact that in this country, an unborn sea turtle has more legal protection than an unborn child? Did you know that everyday in America approximately 5,000 babies are aborted? Five thousand precious and innocent lives murdered. Every third child conceived in America is aborted. One might choose to believe the unborn child is not truly alive, therefore it cannot be murdered, but this is a lie. There are four basic criteria needed to establish biological life: metabolism, growth, reaction to stimuli, and reproduction. The zygote is the simplest form of a baby. It is created when a spermatozoon and an ovum combine at conception. The zygote fulfills all four of these criteria and scientifically cannot be considered "not alive." But the government chooses to ignore this. An abortionist, Dr. Neville Sender, is quoted to have said, "We know that it's killing, but the state permits killing under certain circumstances." These murders are often some of the most heinous and cruel deaths one could imagine. Partial birth abortion, a practice legal in this country, more closely resembles a maniacal homicide than a "medical operation." The doctor delivers the baby – everything but the head which still remains in the uterus. At this point the doctor inserts a pair of scissors into the living baby's skull and spreads the blades apart to make room for a suction tube. The doctor then sucks the baby's brains out through the tube. Had the baby been four inches further from its position in the uterus, this crime would have merited imprisonment or possibly even the death penalty. The only difference in the child is the location. It is like saying here I am a human, and here I am not. How can this be accepted? Another confusing aspect of the abortion controversy is inconsistency of the government. The 1973 Roe verses Wade case ruled that it is illegal to ban abortion during the first trimester of pregnancy. Last year a man in

Missouri shot and killed a woman who was ten weeks pregnant. The man was charged with murder for both the lady and her unborn child. Ten weeks is in the first trimester of pregnancy, the same time frame in which it is illegal to ban the murder of an unborn child through the practice of abortion. How can one say that this man committed murder when the abortion doctors have not? Abortion is an absurd and horrific practice. With its acceptance comes the depreciation of human life and value. If people do not begin to realize what this completely selfish act is – murder – I cannot bear to imagine our future. Once we have lost the value of life, we have lost ourselves.

7
THE GREATEST HERESY
PLAGUING EVANGELICAL CHRISTIANS TODAY

In every generation, the Church of Jesus Christ must face the question, *"What is required for a person to be saved and to possess the assurance that he is destined for Heaven when he dies?"*

Another way of stating this basic question is to ask, *"How much does one have to know and to what does one have to commit in order to receive the gift of eternal salvation?"*

The Church can be wrong about many issues, but if she is wrong about this matter, she guarantees her demise.

I have often heard testimonies like this: "I was saved when I was twelve years of age. I joined the church; I was baptized and very active in the church, but I never really committed my life to Christ until I was thirty-five years old." Others express it this way: "I was saved when I was twelve, but I did not make Jesus the Lord of my life until I was thirty-five years old."

So what about individuals like these who confess they are saved but never totally commit their lives to Christ?

- Are they saved because of their one-time decision of inviting Jesus into their hearts, even though there is no evidence of repentance or change in their lives?
- Or is it possible that these so-called Christians were never actually saved until later when they finally committed their lives to Jesus Christ?
- Could it be that thousands — even millions — of people make shallow commitments based only on

intellectual assent to the Gospel and are therefore not really saved?

If the answer to this latter question is *yes*, then this statement is also true: The people who fit this description and die in that lost state will be separated from God in hell forever.

There is a widespread teaching in evangelical circles today that goes like this:

- All that is required for a person to be saved is that he believes the facts of the Gospel and verbalizes those facts to God in prayer; it is *not* necessary for him to repent and to be changed in lifestyle.
- No commitment of any kind is required for salvation, since a person is saved by simple faith.
- To require repentance — a change in one's life and actions — would be the same as teaching salvation by works. But God says, "Only believe the Gospel plus nothing."

A special term is now applied to this kind of teaching. It is called *"Easy Believism."*

What Is Biblical Saving Faith?

This, then, is the question that must be addressed.

The Scottish preacher, Robert Sandeman, embraced the heresy of "Easy Believism" in the nineteenth century, insisting that saving faith is merely believing the facts about Christ's atoning death. He taught that to require repentance and a change of lifestyle would be a corruption of the Gospel. The result of this teaching was an absolutely intellectualizing of evangelical faith. A Baptist named Andrew Fuller, a contemporary of Sandeman, opposed this teaching, asserting that its propagation would result in spiritual death in our churches.

In our day, this old heresy has raised its head again. Professors Zane Hodges and Charles Ryrie of Dallas Theological Seminary have strongly advocated the doctrine of "Easy Believism," writing that the central issue of salvation is not repentance and a change from one's former lifestyle, but rather a mere belief that Jesus is the Messiah (the Christ) and one's Savior.

Hodges and Ryrie further insist that the conditions of salvation are set forth in Romans 10:9,10 — namely, that to be saved, one must "confess with his mouth the Lord Jesus Christ and believe in his heart that God has raised him from the dead." These conditions do not require one to commit to the Lordship of Christ, but only to profess his intellectual faith in the deity of Jesus. According to Professors Hodges and Ryrie, the confession of "Lord" in Romans 10:9 is an acknowledgment that Jesus is God or deity, *not* the acceptance of His lordship over one's life.

That the "Easy Believism" view of saving faith is erroneous can be easily seen when we understand the way that saving faith is stated in the Greek New Testament. Three prepositions are used to elucidate the Greek verb "believe," which is *pisteuein*. This word is followed by three different Greek prepositions, each of which explain the true nature of saving faith and prove that it entails more than intellectual belief and outward confession.

For example, John 3:15 asserts, "...Whosoever believes in [*pisteuon en*] Him should not perish but have eternal life." The preposition "in" here simply means *in*. However, the preposition used in John 3:16 is *pisteuon eis*, meaning *believing into* Him or *in union with* Him. In addition, Acts 16:31 reads like this: "...Believe on [*pisteuon epi*] the Lord Jesus Christ, and you will be saved...." The preposition in this context means *to believe upon; to rely; to rest; to commit.*

Thus, we can see that saving faith means to believe *in*; to believe *into* (union); and to rest or rely *upon* — all of which add up to *the kind of total surrender and personal trust that changes one's life.* To say that John 3:15, John 3:16, and Acts 16:31 — all classic texts on how to be saved — teach that only intellectual faith is necessary for salvation is to deny the clear meaning of the Greek text.

The meaning of true saving faith was lost during the Middle Ages by the Roman Catholic Church. According to Roman doctrine, one could be saved without any personal knowledge of the Bible or the Gospel. All a person needed was to trust the word of the church as articulated by his priest — that word being in essence, "Submit to the sacraments, beginning with baptism and penance, and you are sure to be saved." The Magisterium of the church had spoken, and its decree was infallible.

By the time of the Reformation in the sixteenth century, a conversation with the faithful may have gone something like this:

"What do you believe?"

"I believe what my church believes."

"But what does your church believe?"

"My church believes what I believe."

"What do you and your church believe?"

"My church and I believe the same thing."

The Reformers, especially Luther and Calvin, did not bow to the Roman church as they sought to define true saving faith. Instead, they went back to the Holy Scriptures. There they discovered that saving faith consists of three essential components.

1. Knowledge of the Gospel

Calvin dogmatically asserted, "There could be no true faith without knowledge of the Gospel." Thus, with one fell swoop, Calvin demolished the Medieval approach to salvation.

It is certainly true that for one to believe psychologically, he must have something to believe. The Apostle Paul cogently asserts this truth in his classic instructions on salvation in Romans 10. First, Paul asserts, "...Whosoever shall call upon the name of the Lord shall be saved" (v. 13).

On the surface, it might appear that one can be saved by mere intellectual belief and confession of the same. But Paul hastens to point out in verses 14-16 that one cannot believe until he has heard the Gospel and that God therefore sends forth proclaimers of the Gospel. He concludes by saying, "So then faith comes by hearing, and hearing by the word of God" (Romans 10:17).

The advocates of "Easy Believism" do teach that one must not only know the facts of the Gospel but must confess such and nothing more. But "Easy Believism" advocates stop short of defining true saving faith. Knowledge is only the *basis* of saving faith; it is not the *essence*.

I am a Baptist minister, and over the years I have watched as thousands of young children, ranging from three to five years, have been baptized in our local churches. One may well wonder how many of these children are able to grasp the death, burial, and resurrection of Jesus.

History does record genuine conversions of individuals who were quite young, such as Sarah Pierpont, mother of Jonathan Edwards. However, such conversions are the exception rather than the rule. It would seem that many children are being persuaded, often even manipulated, to profess faith in Jesus and get baptized and added to our church rolls without understanding the message of the Gospel — not even the fact that they are lost. In fact, it appears that what is transpiring in our midst is tantamount to infant baptism, although by immersion.

Many of our evangelical forefathers opposed sprinkling as a mode of baptism. However, they were even more concerned about the spiritual state of the individuals being baptized than they were the mode of baptism. They insisted that the typical infant is incapable of believing the Gospel and being saved.

In our day, we cling to immersion, even in the case of very young children. Yet at the same time, we are guilty of practicing the heresy so opposed by our forefathers — the baptizing of unregenerate children. This practice contributes to an unregenerate church that includes thousands who are unprepared to enter Heaven when they die.

However, it is possible even for an adult to know the facts of the Gospel without believing the facts he knows. This moves us to the second necessary component of saving faith, as taught in the Scriptures and espoused by the Reformers.

2. BELIEF OF THE GOSPEL

A person's knowledge of the Gospel and his confession of the same do not save him. To be saved, one must believe the Gospel he knows — that is, he must intellectually embrace, accept, and agree that the death, burial, and resurrection of Jesus are true.

Permit me to relate the example of a man who heard the Gospel with deep appreciation but emphatically denied that he believed it. This man was a brilliant engineer in a great computer corporation. He attended a Sunday school class I taught, where I never finished a lesson without explaining the Gospel. Almost every Sunday, this fellow would come to me, expressing the highest appreciation and thanking me profusely for my exposition. In this class, I expounded the Scriptures verse-by-verse, chapter-by-chapter, and book-by-book.

One day his wife approached me with a request: "Dr. Bennett, please talk to my husband about becoming a Christian." To this, I expressed enormous surprise but promised I would visit her husband the next week. I abided by my promise and was received graciously by the man. After I very carefully explained the Gospel to him, I asked, "Does all this make sense to you?"

The man replied, "Yes."

"Do you have any questions?" I asked.

"No," he answered.

Then I asked, "Do you desire to receive Jesus as your own personal Savior and Lord?"

To this question, the man emphatically responded, *"No."*

"Why not?"

He answered without hesitation: "I do not believe the Gospel."

"Do you mean that you do not believe Jesus died for your sins on the Cross, was buried, and arose from the dead?"

"No, I don't."

I responded, "You are the most attentive and appreciative member in my class of 300 members. You tell me every Sunday how you enjoy the lessons."

He replied, "Well, I like to hear you teach. You make it so interesting. Although I do not believe the Gospel, I get a kick out of hearing you tell it."

I then departed from the man's home, greatly disappointed but understanding better than ever the power of the devil, as well as the full requirements of the Gospel. Two years later, I returned to the same man, repeating the way of salvation and pleading with him to respond, after which he gave me the same answer as in my first visit.

This man suddenly died in January 1999 at the age of forty-nine. His wife called me long distance from Houston, declaring with a broken heart, "My husband died in unbelief, although he had heard and known the Gospel."

Two days later, his pastor said to a large funeral audience of engineers: "I wish I could tell you that your friend has gone to Heaven. But by his own admission, he told me that he knew the Gospel message but did not believe it, and Jesus clearly says, '...He who does not believe is condemned already, because he has not believed in the name of the only begotten Son of God' [John 3:18]."

However, even if a person knows the facts of the Gospel, believes those facts fully, and is willing to confess them, this does not qualify that person to be saved. The best way I know of to illustrate this tragedy is to refer to the devil.

Just suppose I preach in my church one Sunday, and the devil is present in person. I give the invitation. The devil comes down to the front and says to me that he desires to join the church.

I say to him, "Mr. Devil, before I let you join our church, I must ask you some questions. Do you believe the Bible is the infallible Word of God?"

"Absolutely, no doubt."

"Do you believe Jesus Christ is the Son of God?"

"No doubt."

"Do you believe He died on the Cross and rose again?"

"Absolutely."

"Do you believe He is the only way to be saved?"

"Surely do."

"Do you believe that Jesus was born of a virgin?"

"With all my heart."

"Do you also believe one must repent and trust Jesus to be saved?"

"Yes, without question."

"Do you know that this is a Baptist church and that to join, you must be immersed?"

"Yes, I understand that and desire to be baptized by immersion. I even saw John baptize Jesus."

"If you join, we will expect you to attend faithfully, give your money, and support your church to the full."

"If I join your church, I will attend every service unless providentially hindered. I want to sing in the choir, serve as a deacon, and give my money to the church. You will be proud of me as one of your members."

After I interviewed the devil in this manner, what would happen if I turned to the congregation and asked, "Shall we accept him?" More than likely, the entire congregation would respond, "Yes, thank God he has made this decision! We gladly vote him into our fellowship."

However, notice that I only asked the devil of his *knowledge* and *belief* in the Gospel. I did *not* ask him if he would repent and turn his life over to Jesus and renounce his rebellion and ungodly lifestyle. Had I made this one of the requirements, the devil would have balked, because he will *never* surrender his life to Jesus.

Don't ever forget: The devil knows and believes the Gospel, but the Bible still closes with that same devil cast into the lake of fire forever (Revelations 19:20). Should this not be a warning to us today not to dilute the full requirements of saving faith?

3. TRUST IN JESUS

There is a final and confirming evidence of saving faith — *trust*. One is never saved by the *plan* of salvation, but by the *Man* of salvation. The lost person must know what Jesus has done to save him; he must believe that these facts are true; and then he must take the final step of trusting Jesus Christ and Him alone as his personal Lord and Savior.

Saving faith is always centered in the Person of Jesus Christ. We are clearly instructed in many passages of the New Testament on how to be saved:

> **But as many as received HIM, to them gave he power to become the sons of God, even to them that believe on his name.**
>
> **John 1:12** *KJV*
>
> **And as Moses lifted up the serpent in the wilderness, even so must the Son of man be lifted up:**
> **That whosoever believeth in HIM should not perish, but have eternal life.**
> **For God so loved the world, that he gave his only begotten Son, that whosoever believeth in HIM should not perish, but have everlasting life.**
>
> **John 3:14-16** *KJV*
>
> **For God sent not his Son into the world to condemn the world; but that the world through HIM might be saved.**
> **He that believeth on HIM is not condemned: but he that believeth not is condemned already, because he hath not believed in the name of the only begotten Son of God.**

John 3:17,18 *KJV*

He that believeth on THE SON hath everlasting life: and he that believeth not the Son shall not see life; but the wrath of God abideth on him.
John 3:36 *KJV*

Verily, verily, I say unto you, He that believeth on ME hath everlasting life.
John 6:47 *KJV*

Neither is there salvation in any other: for there is none other name under heaven given among men, whereby we must be saved.
Acts 4:12 *KJV*

He that hath THE SON hath life; and he that hath not the Son of God hath not life.
These things have I written unto you that believe on the name of the Son of God; that ye may know that ye have eternal life, and that ye may believe on the name of the Son of God.
1 John 5:12-13 *KJV*

And they said, Believe on THE LORD JESUS CHRIST, and thou shalt be saved, and thy house.
Acts 16:31 *KJV*

All these verses may be correctly summed up in one sentence: "*Put your trust in the Lord Jesus Christ,* and you will be saved."

What is involved in trust? Trust is more than knowledge and belief. These two elements of saving faith are basically intellectual. Trust is directed toward one Person — *Jesus*.

1. Trust is *reliance upon, surrender to,* and *union with.*
2. It is an act of the will (volitional). When we surrender, we let God, through His Word, set the terms.
3. This involves turning from sin and self (repentance) and relinquishing the control of our lives to Jesus (Lordship), which inevitably results in a new lifestyle (2 Corinthians 5:17). As the great Bible teacher, Dr. Vance Havner, used to say, "If you are like you have always been, you cannot possibly be saved."

Perhaps a couple of concrete illustrations will elucidate the meaning of trust.

Saving faith can be compared to three stages in marriage. First, there must be *knowledge* — the couple must know one another. Second, there must be *belief* — the couple must believe in one another. Still, there is no marriage until they take a third step: They must stand before a minister and commit or surrender themselves to each other. Until they do, the couple remains unmarried.

A person may know the Gospel and believe the Gospel, but he must be willing to turn over his life to the Person of the Gospel before he is saved. The advocates of "Easy Believism" deny the latter requirement. In so doing, they are guilty of the most grievous heresy — the denial of the only way under Heaven given among men whereby any person can be saved.

Let me share one final, vivid illustration of true saving faith. My mother was visiting me while I lived in Arkansas. The time came for her to return home, at which time I recommended that she fly. She replied, "I don't want to fly."

I asked, "Mama, don't you believe in airplanes?" She replied that she did, adding that she knew airplanes flew from Fort Smith, Arkansas, to North Carolina all the time.

Then I said, "If you believe in airplanes and know that they fly to North Carolina all the time, why don't you want to fly?"

My mother replied, "Well, I do believe in airplanes, but I do not believe enough in airplanes to risk my life in an airplane."

Similarly, many are the people who know and believe the Gospel but who refuse to trust their lives in the hands of Jesus.

Well, my mother never arrived back in North Carolina by airplane. Knowledge and belief in airplanes could not get her back to that state. In the same way, many people know and believe the Gospel but refuse to trust their lives in the hands of Jesus. Just as my mother could not arrive back home in an airplane without trusting her all to that airplane, neither can anyone arrive in Heaven without trusting his or her all to Jesus.

QUESTIONS ABOUT 'EASY BELIEVISM'

1. Why is "Easy Believism" becoming increasingly prevalent today?

   A. **Satan desires the damnation of millions of souls.** If he cannot accomplish this by getting humankind to deny the Gospel outright, he does so by seducing man into diluting the Gospel until it has no saving power.
   B. **The pride of man demands numbers:** Too often the requirements of the Gospel are reduced in order to increase the numbers of outward professions and baptisms. I know an evangelist of great note who at one time preached repentance

and a changed life as prerequisites for salvation. As time rolled along, it became more and more difficult to "get people down the aisles." This evangelist shifted to "Easy-Believism" evangelism, proclaiming everywhere that one did not need to repent of sin to be saved. He said that repentance was only a change of mind about Christ — not about sin — and that repentance would come later. I also know a pastor of note who categorically said that the greatest error of evangelical preachers was to preach that men must repent of their sins to be saved.

2. **What are the dangers of "Easy Believism?"**

   A. **An unregenerate church membership:** There is growing evidence that this tragedy exists in many of our local churches. Dr. George Truett, former pastor for forty-seven years of the First Baptist Church in Dallas, Texas., used to say that 25% of church members are lost. His successor, Dr. Wally A. Criswell, believed that 75% of church members are lost.

   B. **Turmoil in local churches:** People who profess to be Christians but do not possess the Holy Spirit or a new life in Christ cannot be expected to conduct themselves properly when they come together in a local church. Such persons have their own selfish agendas and will promote them through their churches on the false grounds that the church is a democracy, even though it is clearly presented as a theocracy, or "Christocracy," in the New Testament.

   C. **Spiritual deadness:** This results in a form of godliness that denies the power thereof (2 Timothy 3:5). In such churches, evangelism and missions are either nonexistent or so anemic that not even those of junior age are being saved. A large proportion of evangelical churches frequently don't baptize one person during the course of an entire year. How could any church with a regenerate membership keep from winning one person to Jesus in 365 days?

D. **Creeping Universalism:** Philosophical pluralism is the mentality of Western culture. It insists that knowledge of objective truth is impossible. Because truth is impossible, it is immoral to say one religion is superior to another. Certainly no religion has the right to pronounce another wrong. According to this view, the sole heresy has become the view that there *is* such a thing as heresy. In such a world, evangelism is written off as grotesque.

Thus, the climate is ripe for universalism to become a major danger to us. I do not mean to say that evangelicals will begin teaching universalism as a belief. However, I do believe that they stand in danger of practicing it, even while denying it doctrinally. Already the doctrine of hell is jettisoned in most of our churches and actually denied in many.

Dr. Paige Patterson, President of Southwestern Baptist Theological Seminary in Fort Worth, Texas, said to me recently, "The greatest threat facing evangelicals is not hyper-Calvinism but a creeping universalism." A major official of the North Carolina Baptist Convention expressed a similar sentiment to me, saying that he believed universalism was perhaps the most alarming trend among evangelicals.

What has opened the door for such doctrinal aberration? 1) The error of pluralism, and 2) the teaching of "Easy Believism." It is but a short step from requiring nothing for salvation to believing that a loving God will permit no one to be eternally lost in hell.

E. **Deception about the nature of true salvation:** This deception is the supreme tragedy of "Easy Believism," for it is leading multitudes to hell. Jesus speaks of multitudes who possess knowledge of the Gospel and confess that knowledge with their mouths, believing throughout this life that they are saved — only to discover in the Judgment that they are lost forever. These people are not hypocrites; rather, they are sincerely deceived. They make an orthodox profession of faith, calling Jesus "Lord." They may do many wonderful works in His name, including miracles. They are so confident of their salvation that they argue with Jesus in the Judgment (Matthew 7:21-24). Such persons have been deceived by "Easy Believism." Although utterly sincere, they will be eternally lost.

> "Not everyone who says to Me, 'Lord, Lord,' shall enter the kingdom of heaven, but he who does the will of My Father in heaven.
> "Many will say to Me in that day, 'Lord, Lord, have we not prophesied in Your name, cast out demons in Your name, and done many wonders in Your name?'
> "And then I will declare to them, 'I never knew you; depart from Me, you who practice lawlessness!'"
> Matthew 7:21-23 *NKJV*

3. **What is the answer to "Easy Believism?"**

A. The only answer is a return to the true apostolic Gospel as taught in the New Testament, espoused by Jesus and the Reformers and embraced by our evangelical forefathers. This calls for preachers who have the "nerve" to preach the Gospel "...which was once for all delivered to the saints" (Jude 1:3).

B. What is this Gospel? The truth that all who would be saved must repent of their sins, trust Jesus Christ as both Lord and Savior, and show that they have done so by a changed lifestyle.

Does this describe you?

8
Why the War Against Christianity?

The most crucial war in American history is now raging: *the war against Christianity*. This war has been in progress for more than a half century and is now heating up to its most critical point. Will Christians win or lose this war? Mr. and Mrs. Average American hold the answer to this question.

Let us now seek to analyze the war and see what we can do to win it for ourselves, our children, grandchildren, and our beloved America.

CAUSES OF THE WAR AGAINST CHRISTIANITY

1. **The falsification of our history:** Dr. Paul Vitz, Professor of Psychology of New York University, was appointed in 1985 by President Reagan to head up a blue-ribbon panel to examine textbooks used in our public schools. This panel found that almost all references to the religious foundations of our country had been expurgated. As a result, we have tens of millions of people in this country who haven't the foggiest idea where our nation came from or who started it.

2. **The Misinterpretation of our Constitution:** An example is the First Amendment and the myth of the "separation of church and state" (*see* discussion below under "The Course of the War Against Christianity").

3. **The Liberal Media:** Although America has two major political parties, it also has what is essentially a one-party media. More than 90% of all members of the media are liberally oriented. They either disregard or have contempt for our religious heritage. Most are

anti-religious and godless in their belief systems and lifestyles.[45]

Who are the people that control the media? We have a definitive profile given us by a Lichter-Rothman report on the "media elite." S. Robert Lichter is a research professor in political science at George Washington University. Stanley Rothman is a professor of government at Smith College. Linda Lichter is co-director (along with Robert Lichter of the Center for Media and Public Affairs in Washington, D. C. They did an important survey of 104 of the "most influential television writers, producers, and executives," which found — as could be expected — that these were very liberal people.[46]

Here is what they found:

- 93% "say they seldom or never attend religious services."
- 75% "describe themselves as left of center politically, compared to only 14% who place themselves to the right of center."
- 97% "believe that 'a woman has the right to decide for herself whether to have an abortion."
- 80% "do not regard homosexual relations as wrong."
- Only 5% "agree strongly that homosexuality is wrong, com-

---

[45] S. Robert Lichter, Linda S. Lichter, and Stanley Rothman, with the assistance of Daniel Amundson, *Prime Time: How TV Portrays American Culture* (Washington D. C.: Regnery Publishing, 1994), p. 422.
[46] Lichter, et al., *Prime Time*, pp. 422-24.

- 86% "support the rights of homosexual to teach in public schools."
- 51% "do not regard adultery as wrong."
- Only 17% "strongly agree that extramarital affairs are wrong."[47]

This survey shows so clearly why we find an anti-Christian bias in the media. These are nonreligious people projecting their own worldview on the screen and in today's music as well.

4. **The Eroding of Morals in Movies and Pop Music:**

Some of today's anti-Christian films literally feature evil characters who actually kill *because* they are born-again Christians, such as *Guilty as Charged, The Handmaid's Tale,* or *The Rapture.* How perverted and how twisted could Hollywood get? Today Hollywood often glamorizes the bad guy — the moral reprobate — and demonizes the good guy — the Christian. This reminds me of what Isaiah once said: "Woe to those who call evil good, and good evil" (Isaiah 5:20). Unfortunately, much of Hollywood's output violates that biblical principle.[48]

Rock and roll has had a powerful anti-Christian sub-theme for decades now. Madonna, whose very name is

---

[47] Ibid.
[48] Dr. D. James Kennedy, *The Gates of Hell Shall Not Prevail* (Nashville: Thomas Nelson Publishers, 1996), p. 99.

of Christian derivation, seems to enjoy mocking Christianity, Catholicism in particular. She seems able to combine sex and religion simultaneously. For example, in her music video "Like a Prayer," she dances around in a sensual way with a low-cut dress while leading a church choir. She once told *Spin* magazine: "Crucifixes are sexy because there is a naked man on them." It's open season on Christianity in our pop culture today![49]

5. **Humanism in our schools:**

   Have you heard the joke about the teacher who discovered a number of students kneeling in a corner of the playground during recess? She rushed over and said, "Students! Students! What are you doing?" They answered, "We're sorry, we were just shooting craps." She replied, "Phew! I was afraid you were praying!" While that may be humorous, it underscores a tragic truth.[50]

6. **The passivity of pastors:** Don Wildmon, a bold Christian who, through the American Family Association, has provided much salt and light in our dark and decaying culture, wrote an excellent column entitled "300,000 Silent Pulpits" that is worth reprinting:

   > Today, 4,000 innocent precious lives of unborn babies were snuffed out...
   > And 300,000 pulpits are silent...

---

[49] Ibid., p. 105.
[50] Ibid., pp. 121-122.

The networks make a mockery of Christians, the Christian faith and Christian values with nearly every show they air. Greed, materialism, violence, sexual immorality are standard fare. Program after program, movie after movie contain anti-Christian episodes and plots. News articles condescendingly refer to the "fundamentalist, right-wing Christians." Those who speak for the sacredness of life are branded as extremists.

And 300,000 pulpits are silent.

Teenage suicide is the highest it has ever been...

Christian morality cannot be taught in schools but atheistic immorality can...

And 300,000 pulpits are silent.

Rape has increased 700 percent in the last fifty years, and that takes into consideration the population growth...

And 300,000 pulpits are silent.

Rock music fills the airwaves and our children's minds with music which legitimizes rape, murder, forced sex, sadomasochism, adultery, satanic worship, etc.

And 300,000 pulpits are silent.

A majority of states now have lotteries. We have eliminated that crime by making it legal and putting it under the control of the state.

And 300,000 pulpits are silent.[51]

---

[51] Donald Wildmon, "300,000 Silent Pulpits," *Citizen's Bar Association Bulletin*, Vol. 3, No. 12.

7. **Liberal and lukewarm churches:** There was a day in the not-too-distant past when a Southern Baptist church member who had to relocate to another state and wanted a recommendation for a church could be told, "Just find a Southern Baptist Church in your area, and you can be sure of sound doctrine." This isn't the case anymore. Within the denomination itself are found two extremes. On one end of the continuum is the legalist who preaches a "works" salvation, and on the other end is the liberalist who, in the name of "love," accepts everyone and every kind of evil doctrine that is out there — practicing homosexuals, same-sex marriage, abortion, and the list goes on.

This situation is not just found in Southern Baptist Churches but in other denominations as well. In Albert Mohler's commentary on Dave Shiflett's book, *Exodus: Why Americans are Fleeing Liberal Churches for Conservative Christianity*, Mohler quotes an interview that Shiflett had with Hugo Blankenship, Jr., the son of Hugo Blankenship, who served as Bishop of the Episcopalian church of Cuba.

> As Shiflett sees it, the church that Bishop Hugo Blankenship has served and loved is gone. In its place is a church that preaches a message Shiflett summarizes as this: "God is love, God's love is inclusive, God acts in justice to see that everyone is included, we therefore ought to be co-actors and co-creators with God to make the world over in the way he wishes."[52]

---

[52] Albert Mohler, "A New Exodus? Americans Are Exiting Liberal Churches," 6/6/05, albertmohler.com/commentary.

Thankfully, there seems to be a membership decline in liberal denominations. Shiflett says, "Americans want the Good News, not the minister's political views or intellectual coaching."[53]

Citing a study published in 2000 by the Glenmary Research Center, Shiflett reports that the Presbyterian Church USA declined by 11.6 percent over the previous decade, while the United Methodist Church lost "only" 6.7 percent and the Episcopal Church lost 5.3 percent. The United Church of Christ was abandoned by 14.8 percent of its members, while the American Baptist Churches USA were reduced by 5.7 percent.

On the other side of the theological divide, most conservative denominations are growing. The conservative Presbyterian Church in America (PCA) grew 42.4 percent in the same decade that the more liberal Presbyterian denomination lost 11.6 percent of its members. Other conservative denominations experiencing significant growth included the Christian Missionary Alliance (21.8 percent), the Evangelical Free Church (57.2 percent), the Assemblies of God (18.5 percent), and the Southern Baptist Convention (5 percent).

As quoted in *Exodus*, Glenmary director Ken Sanchagrin told the *New York Times* that he was "astounded to

---

[53] Ibid.

see that by and large the growing churches are those that we ordinarily call conservative. And when I looked at those that were declining, most were moderate or liberal churches. And the more liberal the denomination, by most people's definition, the more they were losing."[54]

However, although liberal churches are declining in membership now, they wielded much influence before the public woke up to their dangerous teaching, and they still exert considerable influence because of their age, money, and the powerful individuals who comprise their membership.

8. **The apathy of our citizens:** "The only thing necessary for evil to triumph is for good men to do nothing" (Edmond Burke). The average good citizen is enjoying the peace, prosperity, and pleasure of our times, unconcerned that our country is going to hell.

THE COURSE OF THE WAR AGAINST CHRISTIANITY

The start of the war can be traced to a landmark event in 1947 when Justice Hugo Black gave a decision that was actually written by lawyers of the ACLU.[55] It stated, "There should be a wall of separation between church and state."[56]

However, the words "separation of church and state" are not found in the Constitution. They were used by Jefferson in private correspondence in 1802. Jefferson's term, "wall of separation" "...was an entirely arbitrary phrase, never meant

---

[54] Ibid.
[55] Dr. D. James Kennedy, sermon, "The ACLU and Hugo Black," April 2, 2004.
[56] Pat Robinson, *Courting Disaster* (Nashville: Integrity Publishers, 2004), p. 9.

to convey any great message about either theology or social policy,"⁵⁷ and his ideas were immediately forgotten and not used until 1947.

This false teaching of the separation of church and state opened the door for an onslaught against religion in public life. The Supreme Court removed prayer from the public schools in 1963. Following that decision has been the removal of the Bible, the Ten Commandments, biblical creationism, Prayer and Bible Clubs, and now prayer at school graduations and football games.

The war against Christianity is now being drastically stepped up. Michael Novak, eminent columnist, says that only one group of Americans are publicly mocked and held before the world in contempt *Christians*. In recent TV shows, Christians have been held up as bigots, narrow-minded troublemakers, and a threat to our real freedom. The highest officials of our government now refer to "the un-Christian religious right."⁵⁸

---

[57] Ibid., p. 10.
[58] Michael Novak, "The Revolt Against Our Public Culture," *National Review*, May 4, 1984), p. 48.

WHAT DOES HISTORY TEACH US AT THIS POINT?

We should not forget that before the Germans tortured the Jews, they presented them as the off-scourings of the earth, the vilest of persons, the enemies of Germany and of progress. In this way, the German people were prepared for the Holocaust when it occurred. Is something similar happening in America?

DO WE HAVE RELIGIOUS FREEDOM?

Consider these facts compiled by Dr. James Kennedy, my dear friend and best informed pastor in America on public issues:

1. If a student prays over his lunch (in school), it is unconstitutional for him to pray aloud *(Reed vs. Van Hoven* 1965).
2. It is unconstitutional for kindergarten students to recite, "We thank You for the flowers so sweet; we thank You for the food we eat; we thank You for the birds that sing; we thank You for everything." (Did you notice that the word "God" does not even appear in that prayer? However, our courts decided that someone might just think about God, and that is unconstitutional.)
3. It is unconstitutional for students to arrive at school early to hear a student volunteer read prayers that have been offered by the chaplains in the Senate and House of Representatives and published in the Congressional Record.
4. It is unconstitutional for a Board of Education to use or refer to the word "God" in any of its official writings.
5. It is unconstitutional for a kindergarten class to ask during a school assembly,

"Whose birthday is celebrated at Christmas?"
6. It is unconstitutional for the Ten Commandments to hang on the walls of a classroom. (The Ten Commandments hang on the walls of the Supreme Court and were displayed in public classrooms for 150 years and taught in many schools.)
7. A bill becomes unconstitutional, even though the wording may be constitutionally acceptable, if the legislator who introduced the bill had a religious activity in his mind when he authored it.
8. It is unconstitutional for a kindergarten class to recite: "God is great, God is good, let us thank Him for our food."
9. It is unconstitutional for a school graduation ceremony to contain an opening or closing prayer.
10. In the Alaska public schools (1987), students were told that they could not use the word "Christmas" in school because it had the word "Christ" in it. They were also told that they could not have the word in their notebooks or exchange Christmas cards or presents.[59]

CLIMAX OF THE WAR

The war against Christianity has now reached outrageous proportions, as expressed in three major developments in recent years:

1. **The legalization of sodomy:** On June 26, 2003, the U. S. Supreme Court ruled 6–3 that sodomy laws are unconstitutional. "In *Lawrence vs. Texas*, two gay men say the state of Texas deprived them of privacy rights and equal protection under the law when

---

[59] Dr. James Kennedy, sermon, "As Free As We Were," May 20, 2003.

they were arrested in 1998 for having sex in a Houston home."⁶⁰

As a result of the decision of this case, "all sodomy laws in the US are now unconstitutional and unenforceable when applied to non-commercial consenting adults in private."⁶¹

2. **Same-sex marriage:** "Wedding Day — First Gays Marry; Many Seek Licenses"⁶² was the headline in the Boston Globe on May 18, 2004. The article goes on to describe how more than 1,000 gay and lesbian couples rushed into town halls across the state of Massachusetts to obtain a license to marry on May 17, 2004, the first day of legalized same-sex matrimony.

3. **Proposed removal of "Under God" in the Pledge of Allegiance:** A news flash put out by the American Humanist Association, states that in June 2002, a Ninth Circuit Court of Appeals overturned the 1954 act of Congress, which modified our Pledge of Allegiance. "The Judge acknowledged that the words 'under God' which were added in 1954, were an unconstitutional establishment of religion."⁶³ The article goes on to explain that on October 8, 2002, the House of Representatives voted 401 to 5 in favor of a measure to keep "under God" in the Pledge of Allegiance. This was all brought to bear by an atheist named Michael Newdow. Newdow used his young daughter, of whom he did not even have legal custody, to bring this complaint (that his daughter was being harmed by reciting the Pledge in her classroom) to the Ninth Circuit Court. The case was heard by the Supreme Court on March 24, 2004, and the mother of the child came forth saying that Michael Newdow did not have the right to speak for her child, that she and the child were both evangelical Christians, and that the child loved to recite the words "Under God"

---

⁶⁰ www.Sodomylaws.org/lawrence, last edited July 31, 2005.
⁶¹ Ibid.
⁶² Yvonne Abraham and Michael Paulson (Globe Staff), "Wedding Day," May 18, 2004, www.boston.com/news.
⁶³ "News Flash," 2002, www.americanhumanist.org.

in the pledge.[64]

THE CURE FOR THE WAR AGAINST CHRISTIANITY

The war can be won, but only if millions of *concerned* Americans wake up and get involved.

There are seven specific steps we must take:

- **WAKE UP** to what is happening.
- **CLEAN UP** our lives morally and spiritually.
- **SHUT UP** stop blaming everyone else and not taking responsibility ourselves.
- **CONFESS UP** to the salvation that Jesus Christ offers. James Kennedy says that the problem with those fighting Christianity is simple: They have never been converted. Every Christian should be winning the lost, and every local church should have that as its major objective.
- **STAND UP** for the biblical truths and values that have made us great as a nation.
- **SPEAK UP** for your convictions. Dan Quayle said, "What the media wants and the media demands of Christians is very simply this: *your silence.*"[65] The truth is that we need to get involved on the local level in our schools, PTAs, local elections, school board, etc. We need to run for office. We need to register to vote. We need to write letters. We need to be active members and soul-winners in some Bible-preaching church.
- **LOOK UP** to our Sovereign God, imploring Him to intervene through His people and return America to her senses. Psalm 85:6 says, "Wilt you not *thyself* revive us again that your people may rejoice in you?"

---

[64] Robinson, *Courting Disaster*, p. 5.
[65] Dan Quayle speech at the "Reclaiming America for Christ" Seminar, Coral Ridge Presbyterian Church, Fort Lauderdale, Florida, January 22, 1994.

Martin Niemooler was a martyr under Hitler. He wrote these words after it was too late: "When the Nazis came for the Communists, I didn't speak up because I was not a Communist. When the Nazis came for the Jews, I didn't speak up because I was not a Jew. When the Nazis came for the trade unionists, I didn't speak up because I was not a trade unionist. When the Nazis came for the Catholics, I didn't speak up because I was not a Catholic. Then one day, they came for the Protestants and for ME, AND THERE WAS NO ONE TO SPEAK UP."[66]

WHAT CAN YOU DO FOR YOUR COUNTRY?

"Ask not what your country can do for you — ask what you can do for your country" (John F. Kennedy). This question is not asking what you can do for the State or Federal bureaucracy. Rather, the question means, "What can citizens do to ensure the perpetuity of freedom, the preservation of democracy, and the continuation of our republican form of government?" Before answering this question, let's examine some things that Christian citizenship is *not*:

1. **Being a Christian citizen is not our first priority.** No Christian citizen can give ultimate allegiance to any earthly government (Matt. 6:33).
2. **Being a Christian citizen does not constitute an attempt to impose Christianity on all citizens.** Religious pluralism is necessary in a free society. But Christians do have the right to advocate Judeo-Christian truth in all areas of life.
3. **Being a Christian citizen is not blind nationalism.** "America, right or wrong" should read "America, right or wrong: When she is right, to *keep* her right; when she is wrong, to *make* her right."

---

[66] *Time* Magazine, August 28, 1989.

4. **Being a Christian citizen is not world citizenship.** The trend toward globalism is anti-Christian at its roots.

THE CIVIC DUTIES OF CHRISTIANS

1. **Participate.** Many of our earliest leaders were Christians, including many of the signers of the Declaration of Independence. Obviously, our Founding Fathers did not buy the line that politics and the pulpit don't mix.
2. **Pay taxes (Romans 13:6).** A recent poll reveals that 74% of American people favor more spending on government programs, but 70% oppose higher taxes.
3. **Protect the nation.** One survey reveals that 40% of Baby Boomers said they would not fight for their country under any circumstance. No Christian desires bloodshed, but there are times when free men must fight to preserve their freedoms.
4. **Stay informed.** Hosea 4:6 says, "My people are destroyed for lack of knowledge."
5. **Vote without fail**.

THE CHRISTIAN'S MORAL AND SPIRITUAL DUTIES

1. **Pray.** The Bible enjoins us to pray for rulers and those in authority (1 Timothy 2:1,2). Prayer played a significant part in the founding of our nation. George Washington, Abraham Lincoln, and Dwight Eisenhower were mighty men of prayer.
2. **Be a person of integrity.** Our Founding Fathers said that democracy would work only for a moral and religious people. Character is a must not only for elected officials, but also for the electorate.
3. **Build a strong family.** A Christian has a moral responsibility to provide society with a strong model of family life.
4. **Be loyal to a local Bible-believing, Bible-practicing local church.** From the local church

spring the vital movements that feed Christian patriotism and ensure the development of character, the survival of the family, and the ultimate health of a nation.

THE CHRISTIAN'S RESPONSIBILITY TO A LOST WORLD

I am convinced that God has established America as a launching pad for world evangelization. No other nation compares to the United States of America in getting the Gospel to the whole world. It is my conviction that God still has that purpose for America to spread the Gospel to all the world in preparation for the return of the Lord Jesus.

So if you want God to bless America, *get saved* if you are not already saved; then *seek to win the lost to Jesus* in your own personal world. Use every means at your disposal prayer, giving, and going yourself to send the Gospel to the ends of the earth. And if you want God to bless America again, make the prayer of the psalmist *your* prayer as well: "May God be gracious to us and bless us...that your ways may be known on earth, your salvation among all nations" (Psalm 67:1,2 *NIV*).

CONCLUSION

We are winning the war against Christianity, despite the many setbacks of the past decades. The fighters against Christ, His Church, and His people are doomed to failure. Jesus promised, "...I will build my church; and the gates of hell shall not prevail against it" (Matthew 16:18). Solomon observed, "There is no wisdom, no insight, no plan that can succeed against the Lord" (Proverbs 21:30 *NIV*). The next time you see some vicious attack against Christianity on "Prime Time," think of the following documented facts:

- In AD 100, 100 persons a day worldwide were being converted to Christ.
- By 1900, the number of conversions was 943 per day.
- By 1950, that number grew to 4,500.
- By 1980, that 4,500 had grown to 20,000 per day.
- By 1993, it had risen to 86,000 converts per day.
- By 1995, the number converted to Christ exceeded 100,000 per day.
- By 2000, the number reached approximately 200,000 per day.[67]

The kingdom of the world has become the kingdom of our Lord and of his Christ, and he will reign for ever and ever.
Revelation 11:15 *NIV*

A Sad but Holy God

America the beautiful, or so you used to be,
Land of the Pilgrims' pride; I hope they never see,
Babies piled in dumpsters, abortion on demand,
Sweet land of liberty, your house is on the sand.
People wonder aimlessly, poisoned by cocaine,
Choosing to indulge when God said to abstain.
From sea to shining sea, our country turns away,
From the teaching of God's Word and the need to always pray.
We've voted in a government that's rotting at the core,
Appointing godless judges who throw reason out the door.
Too soft to place the killer in his well-deserved tomb,
But brave enough to kill the child before he leaves the womb.
You think God is not angry that our land's a moral slum,'
How much evil will He watch before His Kingdom comes?
How are we to face our God from whom we cannot hide,
What is left for us to do to stem this evil tide?
If we who are called would humbly turn and pray;
If we would seek His holy face and leave our evil way,
Then God would hear from heaven and forgive us our sin;
He'd heal our sickly land, and those who live within
But, America the beautiful, if you don't, then you will see,
A sad but holy God withdraw His hand from thee.
Author Unknown

---

[67] U.S. Center for World Missions, Pasadena, California.

9
The Five Myths About Homosexuality

Some time ago, a program entitled "The Pros and Cons of Homosexuality" was broadcast on television. One lady from Maryland named Diane called in and said, "I don't understand why Christians keep spewing out their hatred of homosexuality and refuse to have open minds."

The announcer asked, "What do you mean by an open mind?"

She replied, "We ought to accept people for who they are."

Many people in America feel this way, but such a viewpoint is quite invalid. Suppose a murderer murders your family one night. Are you to accept that murderer "for who he is"?

Should we accept the men who blew up the World Trade Center for who they were? How about Saddam Hussein or Osama Bin Laden? Of course we should not. Then what *should* we do? We should speak the truth in love and with deep compassion to those who are walking the path to destruction. This will be our approach as we expose the tragedy of homosexuality.

The best way to explore this subject is to consider the five big myths concerning homosexuality:[68]

---

[68] Some of the statistics used in this chapter were taken from a message by Dr. David Allen preached at Macarthur Road Baptist Church in Dallas, Texas.

MYTH NUMBER 1:
THE BIBLE DOES NOT CONDEMN HOMOSEXUALITY

Michael Piazza, pastor of the largest gay church in America, wrote a book in 1994 entitled *Holy Homosexuals*. The purpose of the book was to argue the case that the Bible does not condemn homosexuality. Piazza says that God did not condemn Sodom and Gomorrah for homosexuality, but for the failure to provide proper hospitality to strangers. He argues that Ruth and Naomi were lesbians; that David and Jonathan were involved in a homosexual relationship; and that nowhere in the Bible does Jesus address homosexuality. He also says that when Paul talks about homosexuality, he is referring to heterosexual people who commit a homosexual act.[69]

Such reasoning is ludicrous. Here is why:

1. Leviticus 18:22 forbids a man to lie down with another man or a woman to lie down with another woman. Such acts are abominable in the eyes of God.

2. Jude 1:7 says that the people of Sodom and Gomorrah were trafficking in "strange flesh," meaning homosexuality.

3. Paul shows in Romans 1 that homosexuality is a deadly sin, chosen by those who suppress and pervert the truth of God.

> **For the wrath of God is revealed from heaven against all ungodliness and unrighteousness of men, who suppress the truth in unrighteousness....**
> **Therefore God also gave them up to uncleanness, in the lusts of their hearts, to dishonor their bodies among themselves, who exchanged the truth of God for the lie, and wor-**

---

[69] Michael Piazza, *Holy Homosexuals* (Morris Publishing, July 1994), passim.

> shiped and served the creature rather than the Creator, who is blessed forever. Amen.
>
> For this reason God gave them up to vile passions. For even their women exchanged the natural use for what is against nature.
>
> Likewise also the men, leaving the natural use of the woman, burned in their lust for one another, men with men committing what is shameful, and receiving in themselves the penalty of their error which was due.
>
> **Romans 1:18,24-27**

4. Paul also commands that God's people abstain from sexual immorality. The Greek word he uses, *porneia,* covers every form of sexual sin, including homosexuality (1 Thessalonians 4:3).

5. Paul plainly states that there were members of the church at Corinth who had been homosexuals and lesbians and condemned to hell, but who were later *washed, sanctified,* and *justified* (1 Corinthians 6:11).

6. One Episcopalian priest recently said: "God used to believe that homosexuality was wrong according to the Bible, but He has changed His mind and no longer believes that homosexuality is wrong." Of course, that priest is grossly mistaken, for God is the same yesterday, today, and forever and *never* changes His mind. However, I appreciate that man's honesty in admitting that the Bible itself condemns homosexuality.

Myth Number 2:
10% of the American Population Is Gay

1. The McKenzie report in 1948 left the impression that much of America was perverted or engaged in sexual

immorality. This statistic was later completely repudiated.[70]

In the book, *Sex in America: A Definitive Survey*, we see that Kinsey's research methods were skewed by his choice to include a high percentage of prison inmates and known sex offenders, both of whom engage in homosexual behavior much more frequently than individuals in the general population.[71]

More recently, the National Health and Social Life Survey performed a highly sophisticated study on sexuality in America and found that only 2.8% of the men and 1.4% of the women said they thought of themselves as homosexual or bisexual.[72]

2. Less than 3% of the males and 2% of the females in the U.S. are homosexuals or lesbians. However, let's pretend that 10% of the population *is* gay. If that were true, would it change anything? Would it make homosexuality any less wrong in the eyes of God? No. For instance, it is a fact that 10-15% of Americans are alcoholic. But would anyone argue that alcoholism should be a valid and accepted lifestyle? Of course not.

Myth Number 3:
Homosexuals Are Born That Way

The theory that homosexuals are born as homosexuals was proposed in 1993 by Dean Hamer in his article for *Science* magazine. Hamer basically claimed that science was "on the verge of proving that homosexuality is innate,

---

[70] Alfred C. Kinsey, Wardell B. Pomeray, Clyde E. Martin, *Sexual Behavior in the Human Male* (Philadelphia and London: W. B. Saunders Company, 1948), pp. 650-651.
[71] Robert T. Michael, John H. Gagnon, Edward O. Laumann, and Gina Kolata, *Sex in America: A Definitive Survey* (Boston: Little, Brown and Company, 1994), p. 176.
[72] Ibid., p. 176.

genetic and therefore unchangeable — a normal variant of human nature."[73] *Time* magazine, *Newsweek*, Oprah, and the general media jumped on this false statement. Four months later, this view was completely denied in the same magazine; nevertheless, the media keeps on propagating this lie.

Although homosexuals are not born, they almost always grow up in situations that cause them to turn to homosexuality. Dr. James Dobson states that there has never been one homosexual boy who had a good relationship with his father.[74]

Still, we must note what Paul says in Romans 1:22,23: *Homosexuality is a choice*. It is when humankind refuses to worship the true God and exchanges His glory for idolatry that men and women begin to practice the unnatural acts of homosexuality and lesbianism.

Myth Number 4: Homosexuality Is a Normal, Healthy Lifestyle

Perhaps the best research on this issue was conducted by Bell and Weinberg. The study revealed these facts:

- 73% of male homosexuals have had more than 100 partners.
- 58% have had more than 250 partners.
- 41% have had more than 500 partners.[75]

---

[73] Jeffrey Satinover, M.D., "Is There a 'Gay Gene'?" National Association of Research and Therapy of Homosexuality (NARTH) Fact Sheet, March 1999, p. 1.
[74] Dr. James Dobson, *Bringing Up Boys* (Wheaton, IL: Tyndale House Publishers, Inc., 2001), p. 121.
[75] [First Name] Bell and [First Name] Weinberg, *Journal of Homosexuality*, Vol. 6, No. 4, Summer 1981, pp. 96-97.

Permit me to ask: Does that sound like a normal, healthy lifestyle? Suppose a heterosexual person, a sex addict, went from one one-night stand to another and had relations with 500 women. Would you say that he is normal and healthy?

Do you realize that a person who is a homosexual is 17 times more likely to be a child molester than a heterosexual person? What about the risk of AIDS? A heterosexual faces a small risk of contracting the disease, particularly through blood transfusion. But a heterosexual's chance of acquiring AIDS as a result of unprotected sex is 1 out of 715,000. On the other hand, a homosexual's chance of acquiring AIDS from unprotected sex is 1 out of 165!

MYTH NUMBER 5:
A HOMOSEXUAL CANNOT BE CHANGED

"Once a homosexual, always a homosexual." This is perhaps the most serious myth of all. Dr. Rubin Fine, director of psychoanalytic training for New York City, says, "It is not scientifically accurate to say that homosexuals cannot and do not change; they *do*."

When we turn to the Bible, we are assured in the strongest language that any sinner can be changed. It is good that homosexuality is a sin, for the Bible tells us that *all* sin can be cleansed away by the blood of Christ (1 John 1:7). Romans 5:20 takes it further, stressing that "...where sin did abound, grace did much more abound."

Certainly the sin of homosexuality, so abounding in our day, is covered by God's more abounding grace through Jesus Christ. Homosexuality is *not* the unpardonable sin.

One of my most faithful staff members, who worked with me for fifteen years, is an excellent illustration of this truth. This man was a practicing homosexual until I led him to Christ in 1969. Recently I saw him again, and he is married and living a victorious life, free from the bondage of homosexuality.

Yes, homosexuality is a sin, and it is also a choice. But when a person chooses to serve the true God, that eternal choice sets him free from every sin of the past including the sin of homosexuality.

GOD HAS A 'GAY' WORD FOR THE 'GAY' COMMUNITY

It is strange that sexual perverts (homosexuals and lesbians) call themselves "gay." But are they really "gay"? The dictionary defines "gay" as "gleeful, jovial, glad, joyous, happy, cheerful, sprightly, blithe, airy, light-hearted."[76] These words do not describe the gay community. Rather than being "keenly alive and exuberant," gay people are often depressed, sad, and low in spirits. Many times they are even suicidal.

But there is a "gay" word, a happy and exciting word for victims of sexual perversion. It is found in First Corinthians 6:9-11 (*NAS*):

> **Or do you not know that the unrighteous shall not inherit the Kingdom of God? Do not be deceived; neither fornicators, nor idolaters, nor adulterers, nor effeminate, nor homosexuals, nor thieves, nor the covetous, nor drunkards, nor revilers, nor swindlers, shall inherit the Kingdom of God.**
> **And such were some of you; but you were washed, but you were sanctified, but you were justified in the name of the Lord Jesus**

---

[76] *Webster's Encyclopedia Unabridged Dictionary of the English Language* (New York: Portland House, 1989), p. 587.

Christ, and in the Spirit of our God.

These verses announce happy and healing words for all those whom society calls "gay." Let us note four glorious truths in this passage:

1. **A General Warning:** "...Do you not know that the unrighteous shall not inherit the kingdom of God?..." (1 Corinthians 6:9). "The Kingdom of God" refers to the rule of God in the human heart. It is the same as being saved in Matthew, Mark, and Luke and equivalent to eternal life in John's Gospel. Jesus said one enters this Kingdom through the new birth (John 3:3,5). One must enter this Kingdom in this life in order to inherit the eternal Kingdom in the life to come. In verse 9 (NAS), God warns that "the unrighteous" cannot inherit this Kingdom.

2. **A Timely Caution:** In every age, humankind has lowered God's standards and tried to make themselves believe that the unrighteous would enter His Kingdom. But God raises the red flag, saying, *"Be NOT deceived"* (1 Corinthians 6:9). He hoists the same flag over and over again in the Bible (Ma thew 7:21-24; 2 Corinthians 13:5; Galatians 6:7,8).

3. **A Specific Identification:** Having issued the warning, God goes on to give examples of the "unrighteous" who will not enter the Kingdom (1 Corinthians 6:9,10).
   - Fornicators
   - Thieves
   - Idolaters
   - The Covetous
   - Adulterers
   - Drunkards
   - The Effeminate
   - Revilers

- Homosexuals
- Swindlers

Many members of the "gay" community claim to be believers and insist that the Bible does not condemn sexual perversion (homosexuality or lesbianism). But in the list above, you will note a clear reference to:

- "Homosexuals" and "sodomites" (*NKJV*)
- "Male prostitutes" and "homosexual offenders" (*NIV*)
- "Effeminate" (by perversion) and "homosexuals" (*NAS*)

4. **Finally, a "Gay" Word for the "Gay" Community:**

Verse 11 says, "And such were some of you; but you were washed, but you were sanctified, but you were justified in the name of the Lord Jesus Christ, and in the Spirit of our God." Paul emphatically states that some members of the Corinthian church had in the past been sexual perverts, as well as fornicators, idolaters, adulterers, thieves, covetous, and extortioners. But then the Apostle Paul announces glorious good news for "gays":

A. **You were *washed*** — according to the divine promise that proclaims, "...Though your sins be as scarlet, they shall be as white as snow..." (Isaiah 1:18). This is the promise to the dirtiest pervert on earth who repents and trusts in the Lord Jesus Christ.
B. **You were *sanctified*** — made holy and set apart for the glory and service of Jesus.
C. **You were *justified*** — declared absolutely righteous in the sight of God on the basis of the work of the Lord Jesus on the Cross.

Conclusion

In all fairness, we must note that there are many other sins besides sexual sins. For some reason, the Church has often majored on condemning the sins of the prodigal son and has forgotten the sins of the elder brother (Luke 15:11-32). However, there are most certainly sins of the spirit as well as sins of the flesh. Paul names some of them in First Corinthians 6:10. Covetousness can send a man to hell just as easily as adultery.

Regardless of the sin, however, we must remember that the grace of God can change a sinner's life. As Paul said in First Corinthians 6:11, "And such *were* some of you...."

It is wonderful how our faith in Christ made each of us, once sinners, into new creations (2 Corinthians 5:17,21). But it is important that we *live* as those who are a part of God's new creation. We are not our own. We belong to the Father who made us, the Son who redeemed us, and the Holy Spirit who indwells us. We also belong to the family of God, and our sins can weaken the testimony of the Church and infect the fellowship of its members. For all these reasons, God issues the divine command in First Peter 1:16: *"...Be ye holy, for I am holy."*

10
THE PLACE OF WOMEN IN THE LOCAL CHURCH

What is the place of women in the church? Should they be ordained as deacons, elders, or pastors?

First, let me say that we cannot settle this question on the basis of our emotions, our feelings, our background, or our logical reasoning. We can't even settle it on the basis of what we understand to be human rights and democracy — and certainly not on the basis of political parties. The only way we can settle it with any satisfaction is to go to the Holy Scriptures and see what God says. When we do this, no one's rights are taken away; God's order is in place; and people are well off indeed in the home and in the church.

On the other hand, when this principle of the God-given roles of men and women is not followed, severe consequences ensue. We can see this in our modern society. Because this principle has been so greatly violated over the past several decades, our nation is in deep trouble today.

Before I go further, let me say that I care for every segment of humanity. The churches I have pastored have been open-door churches where *all* are welcome — men and women, rich and poor, educated and uneducated, those who are well-dressed and poorly dressed, Vietnamese and Cubans, whites and blacks. I have no axe to grind, and I'm not waging a political campaign. I am simply trying to present the Word of God on this subject.[77]

The truth is, we could not run our churches without faithful women. If the women were suddenly withdrawn from churches, they would collapse, for we have far more women workers in local churches than we have men.

---

[77] As I recall, I was inspired to prepare the following material after I had read a message by Dr. Paige Patterson on the subject of women in the local church.

In this day of women's liberation, many say that Paul was a male chauvinist who at one time was unhappily married and, as a result of this experience, remained resentful toward women thereafter. There is also the line of thought that says, "Paul was a rabbi, and he simply expresses in his writings the prejudices of the ancient rabbis."

Indeed, the rabbis of that day did have a very low estimate of women. They looked on a woman as something between a man and a beast. There is a well-known prayer in the synagogue service that went like this: "Blessed art Thou our Lord, King of the universe, who hath not made me a woman." That was an actual prayer in those days!

Equal Before God

However, what Paul wrote in Scripture was not his opinion, but the inspired Word of God. Therefore, in way of summary, I want to make several general statements that encompass New Testament teachings on the specific place of women in the church.

1. **First, the Bible is utterly explicit in teaching that both men and women are of equal value in their personhood and in their standing before God.** Galatians 3:28 says, "There is neither Jew nor Greek, there is neither bond nor free, there is neither male nor female: for ye are all one in Christ Jesus."
2. **Both women *and* men are created in the image of God.** In Genesis 1:27 (*KJV*), the writer is very careful to say, "So God created man in his own image, in the image of God created he him; male and female created he them."
3. **Women as well as men have a divine, eternal soul.**
4. **Women as well as men are full-fledged members of the Body of Christ.** Galatians 3:26 (*KJV*) says, "For ye are all the children of God by faith in Christ Jesus."

2. **Peter says in First Peter 3:7 that *women are heirs together with their husbands of the grace of life.***

All these truths are certainly taught in the Bible. No one who has ever read the Bible would believe otherwise. Jesus held to this doctrine, as did the Apostle Paul. They didn't follow the prejudices and errors of the Greeks, Romans, or even of the Jewish leadership.

For instance, the rabbis said that a man should not speak to a woman in public, not even to his wife, yet Jesus violated this rabbinic rule every day that He lived on this earth. The rabbis also said that a man was not to teach a woman. Jesus violated this rule many times as well in the Gospels. In John 4, He held a long theological discussion with a Samaritan harlot. In Luke 10:42, we see a woman seated at Jesus' feet as He taught her. Such actions as these were revolutionary in Jesus' day!

Also, we see in the Gospels that women had a tremendously important place in the life of Jesus. It was women, not men, who were always ministering to Jesus. It is also significant that a woman Mary Magdalene was the first person in history permitted to see the risen Lord in His resurrected body and that women were the first to bear the news of the Resurrection.

Equal in Spiritual Gifts

As we go a little further in the teaching of the Scriptures, we discover that the gifts of the Holy Spirit were bestowed on women as well as men. These spiritual gifts are given to God's people to minister in the church and to build up the Body of Christ.

In First Corinthians 12:7, we have the clear statement of the Word of God on the bestowal of spiritual gifts. It says, "But the manifestation of the Spirit is given to every man to profit withal."

The Greek word translated "man" is actually a word meaning *each one*. Thus, this verse simply says that the gifts of the Spirit have been given to every person in the Body of Christ, to women as well as men. This immediately tells us that women do have a significant and indispensable role in the local church.

EQUAL IN KINGDOM CITIZENSHIP

Also, when you read the New Testament, you don't get far before discovering the conspicuous service of conspicuous women.

- In Acts 16:14, we find that the first convert in Europe was a woman. Her name was Lydia, and in opening her home to Paul, she became instrumental in founding the first church in Europe.
- In Acts 18:26, we see Priscilla beside her husband, not only assisting Paul but also helping to instruct the brilliant Jew, Apollos.
- In Acts 21:9, the four daughters of Phillip the deacon, all prophetesses, are mentioned. Certainly they had an active part in the church of that day.
- Phoebe, mentioned in Romans 16:1, was a helper to Paul. Later in that same chapter, eight other women are singled out who worked in the church at Rome.

So when we bring together the general teaching of God's Word, we conclude that women in their essence and in their personhood are equal with men. Women are not second-rate citizens in the Kingdom of God at all. They are not inferior beings under God. They have been given gifts of the Holy Spirit, and they have a definite place of service in the church.

But then these questions arise:

- What specific place of service did women have in the Early Church?
- Did women have the same place of service as men?
- Were women appointed to the same ministerial and pastoral offices as men?

I propose to demonstrate the answers to these questions on the basis of Scripture.

GOD'S DIVINE ORDER

The fact that women in their essence and in their personhood before God are equal with men does *not* mean that women have been assigned the same role in the local church. Let me illustrate to you a great principle of Scripture regarding God's divine order. If we could understand and follow this principle in the age in which we live, we would bring order into our homes, into our schools, into our government, and into the church.

Many years ago, I went to the White House and had the privilege of meeting the President of the United States, Jimmy Carter. When I addressed the President, I did *not* walk up to him and say, "Hi, Jimmy! Glad to see you, ol' buddy! How are you getting along?" No, I looked the President in the eye, shook his hand, and said with great respect, "Mr. President, it's a great pleasure to meet you. How are you?"

Did I address him in this way because he was better than I? No. Did I address him because he was more important in the eyes of God than I? No. I addressed him with honor and respect because his role assignment was quite different from mine. In the order and government of God, President Carter was superior to me. I addressed him as Mr. President, and I respected him for his office and for the authority that had been given to him.

We actually see this great principle of role assignment in the Holy Trinity itself. In John 14:9, Jesus said, "...He who has seen Me has seen the Father...." Jesus was definitely saying that He is deity. But then later in the same Gospel, Jesus said in essence, *"The Father is greater than I"* (John 10:29).

It would appear that Jesus was contradicting Himself, but He wasn't at all. In the first statement when He said, "I am the same as the Father," Jesus was speaking of His essence or His personhood. In the second statement, He was talking about His role in the Godhead. As the Redeemer of the world, Jesus had to submit Himself to the Father in Heaven. He had to come to the earth and walk as a Servant to the Father, even unto death on the Cross. Jesus had to become a Man in order to be the Savior. This was His role assignment.

In one sense, the Father was greater than the Son, and yet the Two are the same in essence and in their Personhood. The Son is as much God as the Father is God. For both, there is no beginning or end of days.

DIVINE ORDER IN THE HOME

This same principle of Scripture also applies to the place of man and woman in both the home and in the church. In God's great wisdom and plan, the man and woman have two different role assignments. This is simply the way our world is structured in the government of God.

Man has violated this divine order many times through the ages, but never once has it been violated without bringing great sorrow to the home, to the church, to the school, and to the government. It may seem like the violation of God's order is working for a while. But in reality, man never gains ground when he goes against the divinely revealed principles of God in His Word.

Let's look at this divine order as reflected in the home. Ephesians 5:22-24 (*KJV*) says this:

> **Wives, submit yourselves unto your own husbands, as unto the Lord.**
> **For the husband is the head of the wife, even as Christ is the head of the church: and he is the saviour of the body.**
> **Therefore as the church is subject unto Christ, so let the wives be to their own husbands in every thing** [not just in the home].

Now in order to be utterly fair, you should never read those verses without reading verse 25, because it places the man in *his* place of responsibility: "Husbands, love your wives, even as Christ also loved the church, and gave himself for it."

The greatest requirement on earth that any human being is commanded to fulfill is this divine charge to the husband. God's command to the husband is nothing less than for him to die for his wife. The husband must be willing to put his wife first and to sacrifice himself for her. He is to love his wife with the kind of love with which Jesus loves the Church.

This is the universal principle and government of God: Man's role assignment is to be the head and the leader. Then the wife is to subject herself to the husband as he gives her the same unselfish *agape* love that Christ gives the Church.

It is a certainty that a husband who fulfills his God-ordained role assignment, who loves his wife and sacrifices himself as Jesus sacrifices Himself for the Church, will never abuse his wife, nor will her rights ever be forfeited. Yet many women are being abused today by men who pull out this text and tell their wives, "You are supposed to be subject to me!"

On the contrary, husbands never have the right to use their authority to abuse their wives. Authority must always be combined with the love of God. Only then will a divine balance be achieved and God's order preserved.

WHAT DOES IT MEAN TO SUBMIT?

Four times in the New Testament, God commands women to "submit" to their husbands (Ephesians 5:22; Colossians 3:18; 1 Peter 2:11; 1 Peter 3:1). Those of us who believe that the Bible is the inerrant Word of God know that the words of Paul and Peter came from God, not from themselves. Thus, if we have a problem with what the Bible says about women in the church, the issue is not with Paul or Peter, but with the God who gave us the Word (2 Timothy 3:16,17).

The Greek word for "submission" is *hupotasso,* literally meaning *to rank under.* Anyone who has served in the armed forces knows that "rank" has to do with order and authority, not with one's worth or ability. For example, a colonel is higher in rank than a private, but that doesn't mean that the colonel is a better man than a private. It only means that the colonel has a higher rank and thus more authority. Therefore, submission is not subjugation; rather, it is recognizing God's order in the home, the church, the state, and in society.

God commands, "Let all things be done decently and in order" (1 Corinthians 14:40). This is a principle God follows in His creation. Just as an army would be in confusion if there were no levels of authority, so society would be in chaos without submission.

- Children should submit to their parents so they can be trained in love (Ephesians 6:1).

- Employees should submit to their employers (Ephesians 6:5-8).
- Citizens should submit to the civil authorities (Romans 13:1-7; 1 Peter 2:13-20).
- The local church should submit to the pastor (Hebrews 13:7,17).
- Women should submit to their husbands (Ephesians 5:22; Colossians 3:18; 1 Timothy 2:11; 1 Peter 3:1-7).

In First Timothy 2:9-15 (*KJV*), Paul admonished women to give evidence of their submission in the local church in several ways.

1. **Modest Dress (v. 9):** "In like manner also, that the women adorn themselves in modest apparel, with propriety and moderation, not with braided hair or gold or pearls or costly clothing." Paul does not forbid the use of jewelry or lovely clothes, but rather the excessive use of them as substitutes for the true beauty of a "gentle and quiet spirit" (1 Peter 3:4).

   A woman who depends on externals will soon run out of ammunition. Moreover, she is expressing rebellion against her God-given authority. The word translated "modest" in verse 9 is the Greek word, *kosmeo* (from which our word "cosmetic" is derived), meaning *orderly* or *good taste*. The word "sobriety" means *sound mind and good sense*. This describes inner self-control, a spiritual "radar" that tells a woman what is proper in God's sight.

2. **Godly Works (v. 10):** "But, which is proper for women professing godliness, with good works." The concept of "submission" didn't mean women could not serve the Lord in a very great way. The Gospel confirmed their value before God and their equality in the Body of Christ (Galatians 3:28). Women had a

low place in the Greco-Roman world, but the Gospel changed that.

- Women ministered to Jesus in the days of His earthly ministry (Luke 8:1-3).
- Women were present at the crucifixion, burial, and were the first to herald Jesus' resurrection (Matthew 28; Mark 16).
- Godly women were very active in the Early Church (Acts 9:36; 16:14; 17:4,12; 18:1-3).

3. **Quiet Silence (v. 11):** "Let the woman learn in silence with all subjection." Some women abused their newfound freedom and created disturbances by interrupting the church services with too much talk. Paul warns them in this verse to be more reserved. The word "silent" does not mean women were not to open their mouths in church. This is the same word translated "peaceable" in First Timothy 2:2. The women were being told to be more reserved and peaceable in the church and to defer to the headship of men, but not to remain totally silent. Certainly women can pray or teach or give a testimony in the church.

4. **Respecting Authority (v. 12-15):** According to the whole counsel of God, women are permitted to teach in the church.

- Older women are commanded to teach younger women (Titus 2:3-4).
- Timothy was taught at home by his mother and grandmother (2 Timothy 1:5).
- There is nothing wrong with a godly woman instructing a man in private (Acts 18:24-28).

However, a woman must not assume authority in the church and try to take the place of a man. She should exercise "quietness" or moderation, restraint, and help keep order in the church.

GOD'S CHAIN OF COMMAND

Another reference to God's chain of command in Scripture is in First Corinthians 11:3: "But I want you to know that the head of every man is Christ, the head of woman is man, and the head of Christ is God." Here is the divine order clearly stated: God the Father, Jesus in His humanity, man, and woman.

Verses 4-12 have more to say about the chain of command as God designed it:

> **Every man praying or prophesying, having his head covered, dishonors his head.**
> **But every woman who prays or prophesies with her head uncovered dishonors her head, for that is one and the same as if her head were shaved.**
> **For if a woman is not covered, let her also be shorn. But if it is shameful for a woman to be shorn or shaved, let her be covered.**
> **For a man indeed ought not to cover his head, since he is the image and glory of God; but woman is the glory of man.**
> **For man is not from woman, but woman from man.**
> **Nor was man created for the woman, but woman for the man.**
> **For this reason the woman ought to have a symbol of authority on her head, because of the angels.**
> **Nevertheless, neither is man independent of woman, nor woman independent of man, in the Lord.**
> **For as woman came from man, even so man also comes through woman; but all things are from God.**

First, notice that this passage of Scripture is not saying that women are banned from having a significant place in the church. In fact, verse 5 speaks of women praying and prophesying in the church. That is certainly permissible. However, it also says that women must pray or prophesy in the church with a covering or a veil on their heads.

Why is this veil or covering important? Because in the society of antiquity, the covering of a woman's head signified her submission to the authority of her head, who was the husband. For a woman not to have a head covering meant that she was disrespectful of authority, perhaps even living a loose and immoral life.

You may ask, "Does this mean that women must come to church today with their heads covered if they're going to be scriptural?" No, Paul is not emphasizing manner of dress here at all. He is emphasizing a *divine principle*, not a *cultural practice*. In that day, the woman was to signify her submission with the covering of the head. That would not be true today. Ladies who wear hats to church are no more submissive than the ladies who wear no hat. That practice has disappeared, but the principle remains.

What is the principle? The woman should adorn herself with a modest and quiet spirit and recognize the headship of the husband or the man in the home. This same order is true in the church of the living God.

Look at verse 10 again: "For this reason the woman ought to have a symbol of authority on her head, because of the angels." This isn't talking about the woman's physical head. Paul is saying that the woman ought to act under the authority of her husband *because of the angels*.

What does that mean? Just this: When we come to worship, some guests from Heaven, the holy angels are always present. They're looking at us. They know God's divine order.

Their own eyes have witnessed in the church what should be the reflection of Heaven on earth. They know woman is to be under the authority of man. Thus, if they come into an assembly and a woman is violating God's order by not being under the authority of a man, the holy angels of Heaven are indeed offended.

Paul therefore brings this subject of divine order in church to a tremendously high level. He is clearly not talking about something that is insignificant. This matter is something the angels are concerned about-that the woman recognizes the divine order of the Lord.

I doubt there is any question in the world today, in the church or in the home, that is as vital as this question of authority. The chaos in our world basically goes back to this issue of rebellion against the authority of God. Until we learn this lesson of authority, we remain out of God's place for us and out from under the covering of protection that submission to authority affords.

A Meek and Quiet Spirit

Let us return to a Scripture passage mentioned earlier that has caused much controversy in the Body of Christ regarding women's role in the Church:

> **Let the woman learn in silence with all subjection.**
> **But I suffer not a woman to teach, nor to usurp authority over the man, but to be in silence.**
> **For Adam was first formed, then Eve.**
> **And Adam was not deceived, but the woman being deceived was in the transgression.**
> **Not with standing she shall be saved in childbearing, if they continue in faith and charity and holiness with sobriety.**
>
> *1 Timothy 2:11-15* KJV

Verse 11 (*KJV*) says, "Let the woman learn in silence...." What in the world does Paul mean here? Some interpret this scripture wrongly because they do not know what it says in the original Greek. For instance, a man once said to me, "In our church, we don't let a woman teach, sing in the choir, or open her mouth. When women come to church, they have to just sit there and be mute."

But the word "silence" in this verse does not mean complete muteness at all. The Greek word is *hesuchia*, which means *a quiet and meek spirit*.

In First Peter 3:4, Peter commends women who have a meek and quiet spirit. This is *not* referring to complete muteness or refraining from speaking altogether. If the verse were taken literally, many women in the New Testament would have violated this statement. For instance, Priscilla certainly spoke in the church; the daughters of Phillip prophesied in church; and surely Lydia was permitted to speak in the church she helped establish.

Thus, this Scripture doesn't mean women are to refrain completely from speaking in the church; rather, it means they are to be adorned with a meek and quiet spirit, letting the man fill the role of leader without excluding the very important ministries that women can have in the church.

Paul goes on to explain further in verse 12 (*KJV*): "But I suffer not a woman to teach, nor to usurp authority over the man, but to be in silence." Paul isn't saying here that a woman cannot teach in the church. He is saying that a woman is not to teach the man or be the ruling teacher or spokesman in doctrine.

Next, to explain why this order has been established in the church, Paul goes back to the original creation: "For Adam was first formed, then Eve" (v. 13 *KJV*). Paul bases his premise on divine order, the same premise God uses for His order, in the home. Paul says Adam was first in creation.

Then in verse 14 (*KJV*), Paul gives a second reason: "And Adam was not deceived, but the woman being deceived was in the transgression."

So Paul gives two reasons that the woman is not to teach or exercise authority over the man. First, because Adam was first in creation, he is also first in leadership. Second, the woman was deceived, and the man was not.

Here is an amazing fact that I can't quite understand. Women have more discernment than men. They can read hearts and motives and point out phonies more quickly than men can. Nevertheless, they can also be deceived more quickly than men, and Paul says that this is a flaw that does not permit them to be the head. They simply do not have the necessary equipment in their constitution.

'SAVED IN CHILDBEARING'?

In verse 15 (*KJV*), Paul continues with an amazing but beautiful verse on the role of womanhood that remains a mystery to many: "Notwithstanding she shall be saved in childbearing, if they continue in faith and charity and holiness and sobriety." Some say, "That means if a woman has a child, she is going to be automatically saved." But this verse doesn't mean that at all.

The original Greek actually includes the definite article "the," so that it literally means, "Notwithstanding she shall be saved in *the* childbearing." What is Paul talking about? The childbearing he is referring to here is the birth of the Messiah, God's Son, through a specific woman. Here the divinely inspired writer puts his finger on the supreme role of woman, a role that no man can ever fulfill. Paul is pointing to the fact that it was the birth of this male Child from a woman that brought salvation not only to every woman, but also to the world.

The greatest honor that has ever been bestowed upon any segment of humanity has been bestowed upon woman: the honor of giving birth to a child. It is not only an act close to the heart of God — it is the greatest mystery of the universe. Not a man who has ever lived could have ever given birth to the Messiah. That privilege was bestowed on a woman.

If you bring all these teachings together, you will find an exalted picture of womanhood that you can find in no other religion in the world. You will find that women are equal in their essence and in their privilege of approach to God. They are not regarded as second-class citizens in the Kingdom, and their role is in no way inferior to the role of men, for God's role for each individual is always the superior role.

We have also noted that women received gifts of the Spirit as equipment to serve in the Body of Christ and that women rendered conspicuous service within the Church in the apostles' day. But now we come back to our question: Did women hold the same ministerial offices and places of official appointment, as did men?

Let me ask some other more specific questions.

1. *Do we have any record of Jesus ever appointing a woman as an apostle or to any ministerial office?* None. Jesus appointed twelve men as His apostles.
2. *How about the seventy disciples mentioned in Luke 10?* We cannot prove it, but it is widely assumed that the seventy Jesus appointed were also men who went out under His orders. There is no verse of Scripture that indicates Jesus ever appointed a woman to a ministerial office.
3. *How about the apostolic church? What do we find in the book of Acts?* We find women active in all kinds of service for the Church. But did the apostles who knew Jesus personally ever appoint a

woman to be a pastor, bishop, or an elder? Not one verse of Scripture indicates that they ever did.

You might argue, "But Phillip had four daughters who were prophetesses! And what about Miriam (Exodus 15:20), Deborah (Judges 4:4), and Noadiah (Nehemiah 6:14)? The Bible calls all these women prophetesses. Surely they must have held some kind of ministerial office."

That wasn't the same thing. A prophetess was a woman who received special divine revelation and was able to testify to it; however, she did not hold a ministerial office in the Early Church, as far as we can tell from the New Testament.

CAN A WOMAN BE A DEACON?

Were woman made deacons in the Early Church? Some would read Romans 16:1 and say, "Here is the proof that the answer is yes!" Paul says, "I commend unto you Phoebe our sister, who is a servant of the church…" (Romans 16:1). That word "servant" is the Greek word *diakonos*. This is the word for *deacon* or *servant.*

Does this mean that Phoebe was ordained and held the official title of deacon? To help answer that question, let's look back at Romans 15:8: "Now I say that Jesus Christ was a minister [*diakonos*] of the circumcision for the truth of God, to confirm the promises made unto the fathers."

Was Jesus an ordained deacon in a church? No, Jesus didn't hold the office of deacon; He was a *Servant,* and this word *diakonos* often carries that meaning. For instance, Jesus said in Matthew 20:27, "And whosoever would be chief among you, let him be your servant." The word "servant" in this verse is the same Greek word *diakonos.* Was Jesus saying that if you expect to be a true servant, you must be ordained as a deacon? Of course not.

I'm trying to illustrate to you that, in most instances, the word "deacon" in the New Testament does not refer to an office. Now, in First Timothy 3:8-13, it does refer to an office, but most often the word *diakonos* is a word used to refer to *general service*. If you are a servant in your church, you are a *diakonos*, even though you have never been ordained to the office of deacon.

Is there evidence that Phoebe held the office of deacon? There is no evidence. According to Romans 15:2, Phoebe was a help to Paul: "...Indeed she has been a helper of many and of myself also." But we certainly cannot establish on this basis alone that she held the office of deacon.

Let's look at First Timothy 3:12, where Paul does give the necessary qualifications for office of the deacon. He says, "Let the deacons be the husbands of one wife...." I think it would be a little difficult for a woman to meet that qualification! Verse 12 goes on to say, "...ruling their children and their own houses well." This "ruling" would include the wife as well, for in the Bible, it is always the man who leads the home. It therefore seems clear that Paul is speaking specifically to men in this one scriptural reference to the office of the deacon.

THEN WHAT *CAN* WOMEN DO IN THE CHURCH?

The possibilities of what women can do to serve in the Body of Christ are unlimited. For instance, women can teach in the church. They are not called to teach the pastor or to assert authority over the men in the church, but certainly they are needed to teach in other settings that are under the authority of the pastor.

What would we do if we didn't have the teaching talents of women in the church? Most of our Sunday school teachers are women. And think of all the women who sing in the church choirs of our land! No, this verse does not teach that a woman must remain absolutely quiet in church. It is simply teaching moderation and dignity. Let the woman be dignified in church. Let her be charming, quiet, and meek. But she can still speak and make a valuable contribution to her fellow believers!

Titus 2:4 says that the aged women should teach the younger women and one of the primary lessons to be taught is how to be obedient to their husbands (v. 5). The woman who doesn't know her Bible may rear up in rebellion when she hears that, but only because she doesn't see the beauty of God's order. She doesn't understand that when she takes her God-ordained place in that divine order, she is afforded both a covering of protection and her rightful place in the government of God.

God places a tremendous premium on the place of women in the Church. In fact, some of the greatest Christians in Church history have been women. I will mention just one here.

Susanna Wesley, the mother of Charles and John Wesley, was the mother of eighteen children. She spoke English, French, German, Latin, Hebrew, and Greek, but she said, "My place is in the home, pouring my life into my children." Do you know what that one mother accomplished? She essentially saved England from bloody revolution through the ministries of John and Charles! In reality, nothing that God has ever entrusted to a human being is as noble as giving birth to a child and raising that child in the home for the Lord's purposes.

I have pastored for fifty years and the greatest servant of Jesus, the church and me, whom I have ever known, was a noble woman. For almost twenty years she assisted me in numerous ways, such as teaching and winning the lost, but she was always submissive and under my authority. Though in heaven today, I salute her as a woman who fulfilled her biblical role to a "T" in the local church. Name: Mrs. Ann Curtis.

Godly women do have an important ministry in the local assembly, even though they are not called to be teachers of the Word in a pastoral sense. The chief ministry of the woman, says God through Paul, is not to "run" the church, but to care for the home and bear children for the glory of God (1Timothy 5:14). The home gives the woman the greatest opportunity on earth for teaching and ministering to her children and the saints (Romans 16:1-6).

A woman of twelve children once came to Dwight L. Moody, saying she was called to preach. Looking at her twelve children tugging at her dress, Moody replied, "Yes, I can understand that the Lord has called you, for He has already given you a congregation of twelve to instruct!"

Conclusion

So here is the rule: The place of women in the local church is based on the divine order of the home. That's where it all began, and the Bible is written to preserve this order. In every church, women have an invaluable place of service, but it is not to do the preaching or to be the deacons or to be in authority over the men. Rather, it is to assume their role under God, under their pastor, and under their husbands where God has placed them. It is as the woman fulfills this role assignment with a meek and quiet spirit that she can truly be effective in bringing honor to herself and blessing to other people.

11
IS IT SCRIPTURAL TO ADDRESS GOD AS MOTHER?

In 1983, Westminster Press published an "inclusive" language translation of the New Testament and Psalms. In 1995, the Oxford University Press published a similar translation. "The purpose of such a translation," said the publishers, "is to use language that is non-gender specific and also non-offensive to any ethnic group, disabled, handicapped or even left-handed persons."[78] They billed it as the "politically correct" rendition of the Holy Scriptures.

But there is one question that any genuine child of God wants to ask: *"Is it scriptural to change the Bible so that it calls God 'Mother' as well as 'Father' to make it gender-neutral?"* With no taint of sexism in my soul (Galatians 3:28,29), my answer is a resounding *no* for the following reasons.

1. **Scripture itself forbids that any word of any Scripture be changed.** The Bible is verbally (every word) and plenarily (in totality) inspired, meaning that each and every word is in essence the very Word of God. (Second Timothy 3:16 says each word is *theopneustos, or God-breathed*.) Thus, nothing can be added or taken away from the Scriptures. In this case, we are talking about an addition, since referring to God as "Mother" is to add to the words of Scripture (2 Timothy 3:16,17; 2 Peter 1:20,21; Revelation 22:19).

2. **Scripture never addresses God as "Mother" in any context.** The Bible does compare God's emotions to that of a woman in childbirth (Isaiah 42:14), but nowhere does the Bible equate God with

---

[78] Elizabeth Achtemeier, "Exchanging God for 'No God': A Discussion of Female Language for God," *Theology Matters* (*Presbyterians for Faith, Family and Ministry*, Jan/Feb 1995).

a woman (Isaiah 63:16; 2 Corinthians 6:18). In the rules of language, a comparison (*simile*) is quite different from equating one thing with another (*metaphor*).

3. **God has no gender in Scripture.**

   A. God is Spirit (John 4:24).
   B. God is neither male or female in a biological sense. This is also true of angels (Matthew 22:30).

Elizabeth Achtemeier, a renowned liberal observer on the religious scene, declares, "By thus insisting on female language for God, the radical feminists simply continue to emphasize the non-biblical view that God does indeed have sexuality.... This is a complete distortion of the biblical understanding of God, who is without sexual characteristics."[79]

4. **God revealed Himself only in masculine language.** He used such terms as Father, Lord, King, and Husband (Exodus 20:2; Deuteronomy 10:17; Psalm 74:12; Jeremiah 10:10; Hosea 2:16).

The Bible uses masculine language for God because that is the language with which God has revealed Himself. Biblical Christian faith is a revealed religion. It claims no knowledge of God beyond the knowledge He has given of Himself through His words and deeds in the histories of Israel and of Jesus Christ and His Church.

5. **Jesus, the Son of God, addressed God as Father and taught us to do the same.**

   A. Matthew 6:9 in the Lord's Prayer
   B. Matthew 26:39 in Gethsemane
   C. Luke 23:34 on the Cross

---

[79] Elizabeth Achtemeier, "Female Language for God: Should the Church Adopt It?" *Transformation*, Vol. 4, No. 2, 1987, p. 24.

6. **The apostles of Jesus always referred to God as Father.** Never once did any of them address God as Mother (1 John 2:1; James 1:17; 3:9).

A Personal Observation

It is my considered observation that the move to make God a "Mother" as well as a Father is the effort of radical feminists 1) to deny the headship of the male in the home and in the church and 2) to promote the unscriptural desire to equate the leadership roles of the sexes. It is a serious movement because it represents a rebellion against the created order of Almighty God, so clearly revealed in the Holy Scriptures. It has been made doubly serious because this effort is being promoted not only by secular humanists, atheists, and unbelievers, but by certain churches as well.

Will this effort succeed? It cannot succeed wherever people follow the biblical view. But in places where Scripture is viewed as writings that contain error and that express cultural practices and prejudices rather than unchanging revealed truth, you should not be surprised at anything.

The Committee of the National Council of Churches has compiled this special Bible to remove what might appear to be "male bias" phrases and to treat women on an equal plane with men.

I want to quote a statement from the Associated Press that appeared in the *Shreveport Times*. It was entitled "Father, Son Changed in New Bible Reading."[80]

> New York: A keenly controversial collection of Bible readings was issued today referring to Jesus as "Child of God" rather than Son and calling God both Father and Mother. Brackets

---

[80] A dispatch from the Associated Press, *Shreveport Times*, October 15-16, 1983.

> are used to show that the word "and Mother" are added to the original text. This should be noted. Brackets indicate that the compilers of this Bible are not claiming that these words were in the original manuscripts.
>
> This new "inclusive language lectionary," as it is called, is touted as the first attempt to rethink the language of Scripture as inclusive of both men and women. Accordingly, its compilers sought to eliminate male-bias terms that make women seem secondary. The project, carried out by the National Council of Churches at the behest of member denominations, has stirred a storm of protest that has drawn an estimated 10,000 disparaging letters. Critics charge that it is "an evil scheme and dissection of the Bible."[81]

I do not want to imply that people in churches belonging to the National Council of Churches necessarily agree with this variation of the Bible. I don't think most of them do at all. It is my understanding that only a minority of the National Council of Churches membership favor this lectionary, which was compiled by a committee within the organization.

> The Committee was formed (with twelve members) in 1980 on the recommendation of the NCC's Task Force on Biblical Translation, with instructions "to create for use in services of worship inclusive language lectionary...," and these defenders point out that the alterations are not of the Bible itself but of the set of readings for use in public worship through the year.[82]

---

[81] Ibid.
[82] *An Inclusive Language Lectionary* (1983-85), www.bible-researcher.com.

This latter statement is true; there are actually 209 revised passages. "It is not a new Bible," says Clair Randall, the council's general secretary, "but a sequence of passages to be read aloud in Sunday worship."[83]

Notwithstanding, this Bible includes the rewriting of certain Scriptures. This leaves us two questions to ask:

1. **Are these additions to the Bible meant to clarify the original Scripture?** We have many Bible helps. *The Amplified Bible* is one of the most valuable Bibles I have ever seen. It simply gives additional words to clarify or expand on the meanings of the words in Scripture. If that is the purpose of this Bible, it certainly has validity, as long as all added words are put in brackets to indicate that they were not in the original writing. *However, a more serious question must follow.*

2. **Do these additions (such as adding "Our Father *and Mother*" in the Lord's prayer) add to the meaning of what the original writers intended?** If so, this is a serious tampering with Holy Scripture and is seriously condemned without warning at the end of the Bible in Revelation 22:18.

If question number one is true, if the de-sexed Bible is simply an amplification, then it is appropriate and in order. If question number two is true   if there has been an addition to the original meaning of the Holy Scriptures   the de-sexed Bible borders on blasphemy.

Here is an example of a Scripture as it has been rewritten in this Bible: Matthew 3:9 says, "We have Abraham as our Father" [and Sarah and Hagar as our Mother.] In the

---

[83] *Shreveport Times*, October 15-16, 1983.

original text, this scripture does not teach the added phrase in brackets.

When it comes to difficult subjects like this one, I like to learn the views of some of the greatest scholars in the world. I was therefore very interested in a statement by Dr. Bruce Metzger, who is one of the renowned New Testament scholars of Princeton Theological Seminary. When Dr. Metzger speaks about an issue, everyone in the academic and intellectual world perks up and listens. Regarding the matter of this de-sexed Bible, Dr. Metzger says this:

> The changes introduced in language relating to the Deity are tantamount to rewriting the Bible. As a Christian and as a scholar I find this altogether unacceptable. It will divide the church rather than work for an ecumenical understanding.[84]

Secular humanism is making a powerful attempt to break down the difference between men and women and to cast them both in the same role. However, I am not sure this particular strategy is going to get that far.

- In the de-sexed Bible, the Lord's Prayer begins this way: "Our Father (and Mother)...."
- John 3:16 reads like this: "God so loved the world that God gave God's only child...."
- When Jesus prays in John 17:1, the de-sexed Bible makes this addition: "God, my Mother and Father, the hour has come."
- Here is the way this Bible translates or adds to Philippians 1:2: "Grace to you and peace from God

---

[84] Ibid.

our Father and Mother and from the sovereign [rather than "Lord"] Jesus Christ...."

What is wrong with saying, "Our Father and our Mother" in the Lord's Prayer? What is wrong with adding feminine nouns and pronouns alongside the masculine nouns and pronouns referring to God? God is not a male or a female. God in His essence from all eternity is not a sexual being. He is not male any more than He is female.

However, consider these facts:

- Jesus Christ came as the God-Man, a Jewish male.
- God has assigned men, not women, as leaders in the home and in the church.
- The place of women in the Church is based upon the divine rule in the home.
- All these factors help us understand why God uses masculine metaphors to refer to Himself throughout the Scriptures.

Consider also this point: As evangelical conservatives, we believe that every word of Scripture has been inspired. We hold to the belief that the very words of Scripture, not just the general thoughts were chosen by the Holy Spirit. The Holy Spirit could have easily added the feminine pronouns and the feminine substantives or nouns if He had wanted to do so.

For us to say that we can add to the words that were chosen and inspired by the Holy Spirit would be a serious mistake. The primary reason these pronouns must be retained is to *maintain the respective rules of men and women in the government of God.* Using feminine pronouns or terms to refer to God helps confuse and ultimately destroy man's leadership role by making that role the same as woman's role.

This is really what this matter of the de-sexed Bible is all about. It is actually a religious expression of political feminism. If you were to track down the instigators of this movement, you would find that they are people who promote the feminist agenda and are seeking to give women the same role and function as men in the world. In my view, this attempt to rewrite the Bible on that basis is not just unacceptable, it is an example of tampering with Scripture, which God condemns as one of the most serious sins.

It appears that the de-sexed Bible is another strategy aimed at making men and women the same in function. But to do so is to rewrite portions of the Bible in a way that denies a vital truth taught in Scripture. Men and women are of equal personhood, equal value, and equal standing before God. However, God has *not* assigned them the same role in life.

I do not believe that the editors of this Bible are seeking to clarify the original text. The addition of "Mother" in the Lord's Prayer is not to bring clarity to the words of Jesus; its purpose is to add a meaning to the original text that God never intended to be there.

How serious is this? The Bible concludes with a warning against tampering with Scripture. There are two main ways to do this: One could take away from the Scriptures, or one could add to them. In Revelation 22:18 (*KJV*), the warning is given against adding to God's Word, and in verse 19, all are warned not to take away from what He has said:

> **For I testify unto every man that heareth the words of the prophecy of this book, If any man shall add unto these things, God shall add unto him the plagues that are written in this book:**

> **And if any man shall take away from the words of the book of this prophecy, God shall take away his part out of the book of life, and out of the holy city, and from the things which are written in this book.**

I won't try to define the nature of the judgment God is talking about here. Suffice it to say that it is a very serious judgment and that the de-sexed Bible falls in the category of tampering with God's Holy Scriptures.

Here is a pertinent quote from another scholar. His name is John Mayendorf, Professor of Church History at St. Latimer's Orthodox Seminary in New York. He begins by saying, "Any translation is always an interpretation."[85]

This statement is true in a sense, for whenever a Greek scholar seeks to translate Greek words into the English language, he has to choose the English word that will best express the meaning of the Greek term. In almost every case, there are choices to make in this translation process, and many scholars disagree with each other regarding which choice should be made. This is the reason we have various biblical translations — and, in this sense, a translation *is* a form of interpretation.

Remember, this is a scholar who is speaking. He knows whereof he speaks, and he goes on to say the following about the de-sexed Bible: "But this translation departs from the intention of the writer. It is a deception."[86]

There is a sad conclusion that must therefore be drawn regarding this "gender-inclusive" version of the Bible: It is *not* merely a lectionary for the liturgical churches to read on Sunday morning. Rather, it is a formulization and an expression of defiance against God's order in this world, a

---

[85] Ibid.
[86] Ibid.

modern form of rebellion that has helped bring chaos into our homes and has thrown many, many churches into disorder. As such, this particular version should be shunned by anyone who is serious about serving God according to the divine order set forth in His Word.

12
WHY DOES A GOOD GOD ALLOW EVIL AND SUFFERING?

By Dr. Bryan Sims, Ph.D in Apologetics

Introduction

Even apart from the Bible, there are very compelling reasons to believe in God: the origin of the universe and the origin of life, the universe's astounding complexity and design, and a basic universal morality. There are many other pieces of evidence one could explore such as human consciousness, personality, rationality, and religious experience. Someone may not be persuaded by a particular piece of evidence, but just as the different strands come together to form a strong rope, so too the different strands of evidence for God's existence intertwine to form a compelling case.

The picture of God from these various arguments is that of an unbelievably powerful, intelligent, eternal and moral being. However, what about all of the evil and suffering in the world? Since the dawn of human civilization, people have clearly recognized that the world is filled with problems. Just look at the daily headlines and you will see ample evidence for that. All of this suffering, past and present, give many people reason to regard this as the biggest objection to belief in God. Is this evil and suffering compatible with a good God or does it nullify God's existence? He might be almighty and all-knowing, but is he really a good God?

Obviously, to tackle this question is a big task. It will be helpful to clarify the goals of this chapter. <u>First, it is essential to think biblically about this subject</u>. Unfortunately, many people regard the problem of evil as a complete mystery, something which has no explanation at all. If that is the case, does that not cast a shadow on God? The biggest objection to his existence and He has nothing to say about it? I disagree. I think God knows we struggle with this question and because he loves us, He does shed light. To do so, we must lay aside any preconceived notions about God and listen to his word afresh. If you will, I believe that while you might be challenged, you will see how Scripture makes sense. This leads to my second goal: <u>Second, it is possible to make a biblical case that belief in God is compatible with the existence of evil and suffering</u>. Again, notice I said a biblical case. I am not saying a generic notion of God makes sense of evil, but the biblical portrait of God does. Now, I am not saying that I am going to solve everything for you and that you will understand the hand of God in every instance. That is impossible. There will always be an element of mystery. However, it should not remain a complete mystery. Scripture gives us some foundation blocks to see how belief in the God of the Bible is compatible with evil and suffering.

God and Evil

To begin our discussion, we must establish something very important. Without God, the problem of evil does not even make sense. What do I mean by that? In order for something to be called evil, it means that you need an ultimate standard of good. God is that standard. He has no evil, He does no evil. He cannot be tempted nor does he tempt anyone. That is why 1 John 1:5 says, "God is light and in Him there is no darkness at all." If there is no standard of good, you cannot call something evil--it is just a matter of preference. However, this really makes no sense and does not line up with human experience. To deny that the tragic and wicked events of the world are not really evil seems inconceivable. If someone does, I really think they need to question whether they are a card-carrying member of the human race.

Sadly, if you are an atheist, this is the position you are left with. You cannot say anything is objectively wrong. An atheist can only say that he or she does not like something. Also, pantheistic religions like some forms of Buddhism and Hinduism deny the objective reality of evil. Why? The universe is all one so there is no distinction between good and evil. It is all one. Somehow, it does not seem to square that hospitals are the same thing as concentration camps. The Christian might have to answer the problem of evil, but the atheist or the pantheist does not have to answer the problems of good and evil. They cannot account for either even though they both obviously exist.

Evil exists—but in order to call evil "evil" you must presuppose the existence of God. This truth haunted C. S. Lewis while he was an atheist. In Mere Christianity, he writes, "My argument against God was that the universe seemed so cruel and unjust. But how had I got this idea of just and unjust? A man does not call a line crooked unless he has some idea of a straight line. What was I comparing this universe with when I called it unjust?" (45-46). This is truly a powerful point and one that you should press a skeptic on. If they want to argue about the problem, they must assume God exists. The tables are turned on them. Right off the bat, we see that evil and God are compatible.

However, we long to know more. So God and evil are compatible but why does He allow it? I think Scripture sheds light on this all-important issue. In particular, I think there are four reasons God allows evil: to allow free will, demonstrate his wrath and justice, stir people to repentance, and to mold believers into Christ-likeness. With any evil event, more than one if not all of these reasons may be factors. We should avoid any simplistic answers that we often hear.

Reason 1: To Preserve Human Freedom

The first reason God allows suffering is because he gives us the freedom to choose God or reject him, to obey him or reject him. The 1644 Westminster Confession of Faith, famously says that "the chief end of man is to know God and enjoy him forever." God made us to know him—plain and simple. He was not under any obligation to make us. He did not lack fellowship since God is a trinity and enjoyed perfect relations among the three persons of the Godhead. Thus, God made us to know him.

Because God wanted us to have a relationship with him, he gave us something so that we might know him. What is that? A free will. Two people in a relationship must <u>want</u> to know each other. Therefore, God gave us a free will. He did not want robots because robots are not capable of maintaining a relationship. This free will allows us to seek God or to reject him, to seek good or evil. In order to have a genuine choice, we must have the capacity for both. Though our wills have been damaged by the fall of Adam and Eve, we still have the ability to choose or else God's judgment would be unfair. Lest we forget, not only does God allow humans freedom of choice, he also gives angelic beings freedom as well. Of course, some of those beings abuse that freedom by tempting people into sin and creating false beliefs about God.

Parents experience the joy of having their children run up to them and hear them say "Daddy." They are truly happy to see and want to be around the parent. Another blessing, though not quite as heartfelt but just as important, is when children obey their parents--to clean their room or go potty or get dressed and they obey. Now, if a parent found out that their joy to see me or their obedience was the result of a computer chip the hospital implanted that forced them to behave that way, their actions would lose their significance. The point is that they choose to love and chose to obey their parents. That same freedom can be used to reject and disobey me. Likewise, because God loves us and because love presupposes a choice, God allows us the choice to love and obey him. There must be real freedom or else there is not real love. This real freedom must allow for the possibility of evil.

Objection

Let me deal with an objection. People say that God should intervene when evil is about to occur. He gives us free will but should always intervenes when evil is about to arise. This objection initially sounds good but it is not thought through because it means taking away our free will. If God intervenes every time evil is about to occur, then the choice between good and evil is pointless. We are back to being robots which is not a very desirable existence. And some add that this makes God deceptive because he misleads people into thinking they can carry out an action, albeit an evil action, when it is not even possible. I do not think this objection holds water.

The first reason God allows evil is because he loves us enough to grant us free will. It is important to remember that this freedom is the cause of all evil. It is not God's fault. All evil comes from human and demonic sin. We must not forget this. And we must not forget that God is perfect and holy.

Reason 2: To Demonstrate God's Wrath and Justice

A second reason that God allows evil is to demonstrate his wrath and justice.

1. Sometimes God allows people to suffer <u>directly</u> for their own sins. A man embezzles money from his company and is found out. He loses his job, goes to jail; his wife divorces him, etc. A woman lies to her friends, family, and co-workers. Eventually, people catch on to her lies and it leads to a strain in family relations, the loss of friendships and her job. You see my point. Much suffering comes directly from our own choices. I believe when this occurs, these repercussions are not coincidences but are God's judgment to demonstrate his wrath and justice.

   However, there is more to it than that.

2. We also suffer <u>indirectly</u> for our sins. The opening chapter of Habakkuk sheds light on the matter. Habakkuk was an Israelite prophet who lived in the kingdom of Judah. King Solomon's kingdom was split into two parts: Israel and Judah. Israel was wiped out in 722 AD when the Assyrians invaded. It was now a century later. Habakkuk complains to God about the wickedness of his people in Judah and wonders why God does not judge them (1:2-4). Despite witnessing the judgment of the northern kingdom of Israel, the people of Judah persisted in sin for over a century. God would not allow this forever. In Habakkuk 1:5-11, God responds. God is going to judge the wicked Israelites by sending the Babylonians to conquer them. He allows the Israelites to suffer at the hands of the Babylonians as judgment for their sin. Later, Habakkuk predicts the downfall of the Babylonians because of their wickedness—this of course happened at the hands of the Persians. The people of Judah were going to suffer for their sins—not directly as with the guy who embezzles money

where there is a clear line of cause and effect. The people of Judah would suffer indirectly. However, whether it is directly or indirectly, both come from the hand of God. What point am I trying to make? Sometimes we suffer because God is judging for other actions. He indirectly judges us to demonstrate his wrath and justice. Please understand—I am not saying this is the case in every instance. If you remember the story of Job, that was the assumption of Job's friends. If Job was suffering, he must have sinned. That is not always the case and we are mistaken to apply that universally. However, we are likewise mistaken to think that we do not suffer the wrath and judgment of God for our sin. This is true individually and corporately. Amos 3:6 says, "Does disaster come to a city unless the Lord has done it?" This whole notion of suffering indirectly for our sin explains God's usage of natural disasters such as hurricanes, floods, tornadoes, wind storms, droughts, plagues, and diseases. People have experienced such disasters throughout time, but they been riveted into our minds in the past couple of years because of the recent Indonesian tsunami, the Pakistani earthquake, and Hurricane Katrina. According to the Bible, the Lord is the one ultimately responsible, not the blind forces of nature. The Bible does not mince words on the matter. For example, Isaiah 45:5-7 states, "I am the Lord, and there is no other. I form light and create darkness, I make well-being and create calamity, I am the Lord, who does all these things." Why? Why doesn't God just let this go? Perhaps more than any other part of this discussion, this is where it is vital to think biblically. Because God is holy and just, he will not tolerate sin. We all stand condemned. He has the right to judge us. This is not too harsh. It meshes with the biblical view of God who will not tolerate sin. Therefore, God judges sin through the actions of other people and God uses human evil and calamity as tools of judgment upon our sin. Since God has created all these things which belong to him, he has the power and authority to use them as he sees fit. Since God hates sin, he judges it through these various means. In the midst of such acts of judgment, I believe God simultaneously has a dual purpose. This leads me to . . .

Reason 3: To Stir People to Repentance

The third reason God allows suffering is to stir people to repentance. Luke 13 provides essential teaching here. In this passage, people approach Jesus about a recent tragedy: Pontius Pilate, the Roman governor of the area, slaughtered some Galileans who came to Jerusalem to offer their sacrifices for no apparent reason. Jesus also mentions a second tragedy: a tower in the town of Siloam fell on 18 people and killed them.

Jesus' response is fascinating. It was common in those days to believe if tragedy befell you; it was because you were a worse sinner than those who avoided the tragedy. As mentioned above, you see this viewpoint with Job's friends. Applied to these two recent events, the logic is simple: these people must be worse sinners than others because tragedy befell them. Apparently, the people who brought Jesus the news expected Him to affirm this. Jesus' response is surprising. He makes several points that we must grasp:

First, Jesus blames all of humanity as being worthy of such tragedies—both human evil and natural disasters. He tells everyone present to repent—not just the murderers, adulterers, and thieves. Any notion of people dying in tragedies because they are worse sinners is refuted. People die in tragedies because all people stand condemned before God.

Second, Jesus warns them of a worse fate than dying in a tragedy. He warns them to repent--twice. Why does he say that? To begin with, he is certainly talking about more than physical death when he warns them about perishing. Jesus would clearly be in the wrong if he believed everyone would die in some tragedy. He does not mean physical perishing but spiritual perishing. Jesus and the apostles in various places teach that people are spiritually dead—they are separated by God because of their sin (Luke 9:60; Ephesians 2:1). If they persist in this state, they will experience eternal death which is eternal separation from God. So Jesus is warning them to repent of their sins so that they will avoid eternal death.

Jesus is affirming our last point—that God allows evil to demonstrate his wrath and justice—and goes beyond it. What I mean by that is that God has another reason for tragedy—to stir people to repentance.

Why would these types of events stir people to repentance? Jesus does not explicitly say, but I think the reason is that they stir us to consider God's wrath and justice. They are snapshots of final, eternal judgment. When we observe these judgments in the here and now, our hearts should be stirred to recognize that God is holy and just and we need to avoid his wrath. We need to repent.

This is not some sort of irrational fear of thunderstorms or heavy rains. Rather, these are acts of God where he uses human evil like with Pilate or natural disasters like the Tower of Siloam to jar us, to awaken us to the reality that God hates our sin. Notice how Christ calls the victims sinners and offenders. Psalm 7:11 states, "God is a righteous judge, and a God who feels indignation every day." God feels indignation because people continually rebel against his authority.

Recently, the nation witnessed the sad ordeal of the Minneapolis bridge collapse where numerous people lost their lives. John Piper is a well-known pastor who serves at Bethlehem Baptist Church in Minneapolis. His church is within eyesight of the church and in fact he drove over the bridge the night before it collapsed.

His family has a nightly devotion. The Scripture they were slated to read the night the bridge collapsed was this very same passage—certainly no coincidence. I wanted to share some thoughts that Piper penned about the bridge collapse and its relation to evil. Piper resonates with the thrust of Jesus' teaching: "The meaning of the collapse of this bridge is that John Piper is a sinner and should repent or forfeit his life forever. That means I should turn from the silly preoccupations of my life and focus my mind's attention and my heart's affection on God and embrace Jesus Christ as my only hope for the forgiveness of my sins and the hope of eternal life. That is God's message in the collapse of this bridge. That is his most merciful message: there is still time to turn from sin and unbelief and destruction for those of us who live. If we could see the eternal calamity from which he is offering escape we would hear this as the most important message in the world." www.desiringgod.org/Blog/745_putting_my_daughter_to_bed_two_hours_after_the_bridge_collapsed/[88]

We see that such calamities do stir the hearts of many. After 9-11, the nation was genuinely shaken and many people were seeking answers. With the tsunami, it has led to the advance in the gospel as Christian missionaries have walked through doors opened by the disaster. In Thailand, where Christianity is a very small percentage of the population, one village leader said, "The tsunami was a tragedy, but for us it brought new hope. If it had never come, we wouldn't know about Jesus" (Dec 2005, SBC Life, 3).

God is not evil but he allows us to experience evil in response to our actions. It must be stressed—these judgments are a result of our rebellion. In that light, God is not guilty of evil. He has the right to judge his creatures since he made us and maintains a perfect standard by which we are to live.

Some may not like the picture given of God. Let me challenge you with this, if you think God exists, you have three possible routes for explaining these calamities. Either God cannot prevent them or he can but he chooses not to. These choices are both unappealing and unbiblical. The third possibility is that God allows them for reasons given thus far.

Now, let us shift our focus to just believers as we look at the fourth reason God allows evil and suffering: to create greater Christ-likeness. So just to be clear, we are focusing on the Christian and God's usage of suffering to grow them in Christ-likeness. Let us look at this now.

---

[88] Website

Reason 4: To Create Greater Christ-Likeness

C. S. Lewis has famously said: "Pain is God's megaphone to get our attention." Why is this true? As believers, when we get comfortable we have a tendency to forget God, to lose our zeal and passion for him. Not everyone, but in most cases. God uses suffering to get our attention.

Some people reject this idea because they believe that God only wants them to be happy. A very famous quarterback allegedly explained to his soon-to-be-ex second wife why he had an affair: "God wants me to be happy." I believe many people share his sentiments. God is there to make you happy. As I said earlier, if that is your view of God, you will have a hard time explaining why evil exists other than God cannot stop it or does not want to. However, if you believe God can stop suffering and wants to, then you are left with the choice that he has a reason for it. The reason is that He knows that our holiness is more important than our happiness.

God's ultimate purpose for believers is Christ-likeness. Romans 8:28-29 says, "And we know that for those who love God all things work together for good, for those who are called according to his purpose. For those whom he foreknew he also predestined to be conformed to the image of his Son, in order that he might be the firstborn among many brothers." God is orchestrating all things for believers—not for unbelievers—according to his purpose. And what is his purpose? Our goal is Christ-likeness and suffering produces that.

God's Discipline

Now, when we say God creates greater Christ-likeness, I think there are two ways in particular that God accomplishes this. <u>First, God uses evil and suffering to discipline us</u>. Though we might know the Lord and be growing in our relationship with Christ, all of us struggle with sin in varying degrees, whether sins of omission or commission, overt or subtle. So what? Sin, of course, impedes our relationship with Christ. Because God loves us, He does not allow us to remain comfortable in our sin but disciplines us. In the NT book of Hebrews, the writer draws a comparison between earthly fathers and our heavenly Father. In 12:9-11, he writes, "We have had earthly fathers who disciplined us and we respected them. Shall we not much more be subject to the Father of spirits and live? For they disciplined us for a short time as it seemed best to them, but he disciplines us for our good, that we may share his holiness. For the moment all discipline seems painful rather than pleasant, but later it yields the peaceful fruit of righteousness to those who have been trained by it."

Some children love to run across parking lots, but their parents do not share that same love. Because the parents love their children, they do not leave them alone but discipline them. God disciplines us too because he loves us. If someone has a tendency to lie, they will eventually get caught. If someone brags about themselves, they will get humbled. God orchestrates circumstances to discipline you.

More than likely, God will expose your sin—not because he hates you but because He wants to free you from the bondage of sin. Even if you avoid some direct consequence of sin, God will plague your conscience and make you miserable. Your conscience is your red flag to warn you about offending God. When things weigh on your conscience for some time, more than likely by God, you have sin that needs to be confessed. It is amazing how confessing eases our conscience and renews fellowship with God. Paul says in Acts 24:16: "I always take pains to have a clear conscience toward both God and man."

One way God uses evil and suffering is to discipline us so that we will repent of sin. A second way God uses evil and suffering is to test us.

God's Testing

Unlike with discipline, the suffering we endure is not necessarily because of our sin. It is important to distinguish between testing and tempting. Testing is aimed at spiritual maturity. Tempting is aimed at spiritual destruction. God tests but does not tempt. Every time God tests he intends you to obey and grow spiritually. A classic passage concerning this truth is James 1:2-4: "Count it all joy, my brothers, when you meet trials of various kinds, for you know that the testing of your faith produces steadfastness. And let steadfastness have its full effect, that you may be perfect and complete, lacking in nothing." James commands his readers to count it all joy when they face various trials. Why? Because through these trials come greater steadfastness to seek and obey God and from steadfastness comes greater perfection as you desire God more and more. You will not reach perfection in this lifetime but that is the goal that we are striving after. Testing produces that.

Why is suffering so effective for our spiritual growth, whether it be from discipline or testing? You probably already know this. Very simply, they make us more dependent upon God. They make us seek him and long for his presence and guidance. The testimonies of people I have met and read about almost unanimously agree that their times of most intimate relations with God come during the most difficult times.

Advance of the Kingdom

I think it is also worth mentioning that suffering has spurred on the greatest growth in the church. It grew a lot in Jerusalem, but it did not spread across the Roman Empire until it underwent heavy persecution as described in Acts 8. During the years, as the church experienced different waves of persecution, that was when it experienced tremendous growth. The early church leader named Tertullian famously said, "The blood of the martyrs is the seed of the church." In other words, suffering produces spiritual and numerical growth in the church. This was not just in the early church.

It still holds true today. Where is the church growing the fastest in the world? In areas where believers experience hardship. Why does the church grow when it suffers? The reason is the same as our own personal spiritual growth. As Christians mature, the kingdom will advance By the way, the area of slowest growth is the western world. Why do you think that is?

Jesus' Death and Resurrection

I have given four reasons why God allows evil and suffering: to preserve free will, stir hearts toward repentance, and for the believer, to mold us into greater Christ-likeness. These are solid reasons and by themselves, I believe provide a cogent, logical explanation for why God allows suffering. However, from a biblical perspective, something more is needed—Jesus Christ and his death and resurrection which is integral to understanding the problem of evil. In particular, Jesus helps to demonstrate three qualities of God to cement our trust in him.

The Love of God

Someone might say, "It is easy to allow others to suffer, even if for good reasons. How come God doesn't suffer?" I do not think that God had to suffer—he did not owe us anything. It was our own mess. However if he did, it would show us something about the character of God. This is what we see.

Christ, in particular, demonstrates the love of God as no one else. Jesus left the glory and splendor of heaven. He took on a human body and nature with its limitations of pain, hunger, thirst, and fatigue. He endured hardships and persecutions because of his ministry. He died on the cross. In John 15:13, Jesus said, "Greater love has no one than this, that someone lays down his life for his friends." As amazing as it is to die for another person, especially the kind of death Jesus died, we know there was much more going on than that. He suffered the wrath of God on our behalf so that we might be reconciled to God. 2 Corinthians 5:21 says, "For our sake he made him to be sin who knew no sin so that in him we might become the righteousness of God." By his atoning sacrifice, Jesus offers each person an opportunity to experience the love and grace of God.

Also, the love of God is shown in the actions of the Father who loves this evil, rebellious world so much that he sent his Son to die on our behalf (John 3:16). I think we take the power of the Father's sacrifice for granted. Alvin Plantinga is one of the world's most famous philosophers and a Christian. He writes some poignant words, "As the Christian sees things, God does not stand idly by, coolly observing the suffering of his creatures. He enters into and shares our suffering. He endures the anguish of seeing his son, the second person of the Trinity, consigned to the bitterly cruel and shameful death of the cross. Some theologians claim that God cannot suffer. I believe they are wrong. God's capacity for suffering, I believe is proportional to his greatness; it exceeds our capacity for suffering in the same measure as his capacity for knowledge exceeds ours. Christ was prepared to endure the agonies of hell itself; and God, the Lord of the universe, was prepared to accept this suffering in order to overcome sin, and death, and the evils that afflict our world, and to confer on us a life more glorious that we can imagine." (cited in William Lane Craig and J. P. Moreland, Philosophical Foundations for a Christian Worldview, 551). This is no "stand aloof" God or a God utterly removed from creation. This is a God who cares far more about his creation than we do and is willing to take the evil and suffering upon himself and reconcile the world to himself. From a biblical perspective, we should not wonder whether or not God loves us. Romans 5:8 says, "God shows his love toward us in that while we were still sinners, Christ died for us."

The Justice of God

Some might also wonder about all of the evil that apparently people get away with. Murder trials when people appear to go free? Or madmen like Saddam Hussein killing hundreds of thousands of people? Do not these things call into question God's justice?

Once again, we need to go back to the cross where we see the justice of God. What do I mean by that? Because God is perfectly just, he will not simply sweep sin under the rug—he will not simply forgive sin—he must exercise his justice and punish our sin. Jesus died to satisfy the justice of God. If there was any other way to satisfy God's justice, do you think Jesus would have endured such suffering?

Therefore, since the justice of God did not spare Christ, it will not spare sinners either. Romans 14:12 says, "So then each of us will give an account of himself to God." The cross shows how seriously God takes evil. God will have the last say.

The Sovereignty of God

Finally, people wonder can God rid the world of evil and establish goodness forever. Will evil always exist? Again, let us go back to Jesus and his cross. The cross was not an accident but the culmination of God's eternal plan to redeem the world. Acts 2:23 says that Jesus was "delivered up according to the definite plan and foreknowledge of God." The cross could have been thwarted at any point if God so desired. Do you remember Jesus' words to Peter when Peter wanted to fight the soldiers at Jesus' words? Jesus said, "Do you think that I cannot appeal to My Father, and he will at once send me more than twelve legions of angels? (Matthew 26:53)." God was in total control of the situation, even with Satan.

We know from the book of Job that Satan does nothing without God allowing him. It was at the cross that Jesus dealt a death blow to Satan. In John 12:31, Jesus says, "Now is the judgment of this world; now will the ruler of this world be cast out." Later in 16:11, Jesus says, "The ruler of this world is judged." God has given Jesus all authority in the universe as it says in Matthew 28:18 to advance the kingdom of God which has been growing ever since and will one day reach its culmination when Christ returns. At that point, as Revelation 20 teaches, Satan along with his demons will be crushed by Christ and cast into hell forever. Evil will finally be ended.

You say, "How can we know that?" That sounds good but very abstract. It does except for the tangible proof that Jesus gave by rising from the dead. Jesus' resurrection shows that he has all power over death, evil, and demonic power. Because he has such power, we can trust his promises to vanquish these things for all of eternity.

Ultimately, not just Satan will be removed but all forms of suffering. When will that occur? Revelation 21:4 says, "He will wipe away every tear from their eyes, and death shall be no more, neither shall there be mourning nor crying nor pain anymore, for the former things have passed away." I think we all long for a day when we will no longer suffer.

No answer for the problem of evil is complete without a lasting picture of hope.

The Scriptures give us a rock on which to deal with the problem of evil. If someone is grounded in the Lord, he will be able to withstand the worst calamities. Robert Rogers was an electrical engineer who lived in Kansas City. He was married to his wife Melissa for 13 years in what he called was a fairy tale romance. They had four kids, three of them biological and an adopted little girl from China. They were a strong Christian family that placed a high value on their family. Though they lived a blessed life, they experienced their share of trials. One of their kids was born with Down's syndrome, they had two miscarriages including one that was nearly fatal to Melissa, and their baby girl from China was a special needs baby because of a heart condition. As Robert says on his website: "Life was never easy and money was never plentiful, but God was always good and family was so much fun. Perhaps our special-needs children taught us to appreciate the little things in life so profoundly. We treated family moments (and pictures) as something sacred to behold and treasure."

On August 30, 2003, their family was driving home at night from a family wedding when they were caught in a flash flood six feet high and hundreds of feet wide. Robert kicked out the driver's window, but unfortunately he, his wife and youngest child were instantly flushed out of the van—his three youngest were still buckled in their car seats. Sadly, Robert was the only one of his family to survive.

Robert writes, "When I was drowning with my family underwater in the darkness, I could literally sense the peace of God assuring me that they were all going to Heaven and that it was all going to be OK. There was no pain. There was no fear. I continued to simply trust God. Somehow, He pulled me above the rapids and over to the shore . . . I was the only survivor. Even as I identified each of their cold, wet bodies, I had peace through the pain and tears – because of Jesus. He conquered death and removed the sting. In the worst moment of my life, God's presence was the sweetest it's ever been . . . God blessed our family with sweet fillings and a life of "No Regrets." His purpose through me is not finished yet. I believe I miraculously survived and am alive to tell the remarkable testimony of hope and God's grace through tragedy. God can bring beauty from ashes. There is peace through Jesus. God is still good, all the time" (www.mightyintheland.com/index.cfm?PAGE_ID=45)[89]. I can think of no greater tragedy than losing one's family. Rogers' incredible perspective is not because he is a positive person, but because he embraces the truths and promises of Scripture—they are alive to him and a rock to his beaten and battered soul.

Application
Personal Preparation

This leads me to my first point of application. Let me speak to you about dealing with this issue yourself, not just in your interactions with others. Ingrain it in your mind that God is in control of all things, that he is good, and that he does allow you to suffering so that you will become more like Christ. Remember that with every instance of evil and suffering, God is trying to teach and grow you. These are never haphazard but always opportunities of growth. We should not say, "Why me?" but "How do you want me to grow like Christ?"

Let me urge that now is the time to imbed these truths in your heart. When calamity hits is not the time because your heart will be torn in a million ways. Prepare yourself now. These biblical truths I have been expounding have tremendous practical value for your life. They can be an anchor for your soul when it seems the world is caving in around you. We can trust God. 1 Peter 4:19 says, "Therefore let those who suffer according to God's will entrust their souls to a faithful Creator while doing good." If we will remember that truth, we can truly say, "God is good all the time."

Intellectual Problem of Evil

Also, I want to make a couple of applications in dealing with others about the problem of evil and suffering. It is important to realize the distinction between the intellectual

---

[89] Website

and the emotional problems of evil and suffering. The intellectual problem deals with the apparent logical difficulty of an all-powerful, knowing, and loving God with the existence of evil. As we have seen, belief in the existence of God and evil are not contradictory. In fact, you have to believe in God even to be able to call something categorically evil. We have also seen that there are solid reasons for God allowing the problem of evil. All of this to say, there really is no intellectual problem of evil. As a Christian, you need to be prepared to answer this question. I have given you arguments to equip yourself. And as Christians, you should not be apologetic about why evil exists. We do not need to feel like God has messed up or is not in control.

Emotional Problem of Evil

With that said, let me move to the emotional problem of evil which deals with people's doubt or rejection of God because of what they have experienced. In these cases, you might answer all of their intellectual objections. However, that is not what they need at the moment. If your co-worker looks gloomy and you ask him if there is anything wrong, and he tells you his wife just got diagnosed with breast cancer. Now is not the time to unload a bunch of reasons why God allowed this to happen. The Bible says "to weep with those who weep." At these times, people need a shoulder to cry on or a prayer on their behalf. However, eventually, though, they might seek the intellectual reasons so that they can better understand the mind of God. You should be prepared for that. Just remember, people deal with the emotional problem of evil just as much, if not more, than the intellectual problem.

Conclusion

In closing, it deserves mentioning that we should be careful in putting God on trial. God has created the world along with us. He has a right to govern as he wishes. Some people are horribly deficient in music. They have never mastered any instruments, never taken any lessons, and cannot even read music. What would it look like for such a person to walk into a graduate school of music in New York City and start instructing the class? Or to walk up to the conductor of a world famous orchestra and tell him that he does not know what he or she is doing? Sheer madness.

When we are in the presence of someone whose knowledge and skill in a subject far exceeds us, we are wise to keep our mouths shut. How much more when this applies to God? His knowledge of the universe and how to run it is infinitely beyond us. After questioning God throughout his ordeal, at the end of the book God strongly reminds Job that he is God and Job is not.

It is vital to remember that the mind of God far surpasses our capacity to grasp these things. Why God allows suffering will always remain somewhat of a mystery to us, but did you know that it is not a mystery to God. God is not up there trying to figure out how to make it look acceptable. In other words, we have already discussed some pretty compelling reasons that God allows evil, in my opinion enough by itself to rest assured. However, we need to also realize that given the fact that we are so limited and that God is so unlimited, how can we say that God does not have good reasons for allowing evil? God may have thousands of reasons not just the handful I have given. I would imagine that we have not even scratched the surface of God's mind.

We can trust the Lord. If he has revealed solid reasons for allowing evil, we certainly can rest assured that his infinite knowledge and goodness has reasons far exceeding our present knowledge. A beautiful rug may look rough and knotty from the underside, but beautiful from the intended viewing angle. Likewise, the present world looks rough and knotty, but from God's perspective, it looks like a grand tapestry that he has woven together. As the apostle Paul, a man of profound intellect, humbly acknowledged, "Oh, the depth of the riches and wisdom and knowledge of God! How unsearchable are his judgments and how inscrutable his ways! For who has known the mind of the Lord, or who has been his counselor? Or who has given a gift to him that he might be repaid? For from him and through him and to him are all things. To him be glory forever. Amen" (Romans 11:33-36).

13
Who Killed Jesus?

Perhaps you think you know the answer to the question posed by this chapter title. I suspect that most people might glibly say, "It's very obvious who killed Jesus — the *Jews* killed Jesus." But people who would say this have a very shallow understanding of the Cross.

Five theories have been advanced through the centuries as to who killed Jesus, all of which are wrong:

1. The first theory is the one already mentioned — *that the Jews killed Jesus*. It is certainly true that the Jews "engineered" the death of Jesus; however, the Jews were not the power behind the Crucifixion at all.
2. A second theory is that *the Romans killed Jesus*. Certainly the Romans were the immediate instruments of the murder. They scourged His body; they nailed the nails; and they drove the stakes. As it were, they were the people who "pulled the switch," But the Romans were *not* the power behind the Crucifixion.
3. A third theory is that *Jesus committed suicide*. This theory is too absurd for me to answer, so I will move on.
4. A fourth theory is that *Jesus died of physical pain*. This is a perfectly natural explanation, but it is not true in the case of Jesus. The Gospels make it clear that Jesus never lost control of His body. Rather, He was in complete control of His life until He chose to offer it up. Matthew 27:50 (*KJV*) says that Jesus "yielded up the ghost." However, the Greek word for "yielded up" is *aphiemi*, which literally means that Jesus *dismissed* or *sent away* His spirit. Both Mark 15:37 and Luke 23:46 state this same truth. Jesus Himself said in essence, "No man takes my life from Me. I can take it up or lay it down of Myself" (John 10:18).

5. A fifth theory is that *the devil killed Jesus*. This is the biggest lie of all, for, in reality, the opposite is true. Colossians 2:15 says that, on the Cross, Jesus stripped the devil and his demons of all their power, making a public spectacle of them and taking them as captives.

Who killed Jesus? Not the Jews, the Romans, not suicide, not physical pain, and not the devil. I speak reverently and with great mystery, but I speak with the total warrant of the Holy Scriptures. *The great God of Heaven the all-loving Father, as we call Him predestined the death of Jesus Christ on the Cross from all eternity, offering His Son on Calvary's Cross on the plain of human history 2,000 years ago.*

The Cross was *God's* idea, not man's. The Cross was not a temporary measure it was an eternal measure of the Eternal God. When man sinned, it did not catch God by surprise. He had already planned the Cross before He ever created the earth or mankind. In the mind of God, Jesus, the spotless Lamb, "...was slain before the foundation of the world" (Revelation 13:8).

The Jews engineered Jesus' death, and the Romans did the dirty work. But Scripture says that both of these groups were unconsciously fulfilling the determinate counsel and foreknowledge of God. Does that mean the Jews and Romans were not guilty of their ghastly acts? Indeed, no they must answer to God. But the Crucifixion was *not* in the hands of the Jews or the Romans; it was in the hands of the Father in Heaven.

The following scriptures clearly answer our question: "Who killed Jesus?"

1. Revelation 13:8 states that Jesus is "...the Lamb slain from the foundation of the world."

2. Isaiah 53:6 (*NIV*) says, "...The Lord has laid on Him [caused to strike upon Him] the iniquities of us all."
3. Isaiah 53:10 (*NKJV*) states, "...It pleased the Lord to bruise Him; the Lord has put Him to grief."
4. First Peter 1:18-20 says that Jesus was chosen to die before the creation of the world, although the actual Crucifixion occurred in time.
5. Second Corinthians 5:21 notes that God the Father, not human beings, made Jesus to become sin (a sin offering) for you and me.
6. Acts 4:13-18 states that wicked men carried out the Crucifixion, which God had determined from eternity past.

But there is another side to the coin. Although the Father predestined Jesus' death and delivered Him over to the enemy to be crucified, *it was our personal sins that made Jesus' death necessary.*

Do you realize that Jesus never would have died, had it not been for us? He did not die for Himself; He did not die for the Holy Spirit; and He did not die for the Father. There would have been no Cross, had it not been for our sins. Just think of that. The Scriptures are so clear that it was our sin that killed God's Son.

The contemporaries of Jesus Christ looked upon Him on that Cross, and even preceding the Cross, and they saw His terrible suffering. They said, "Here is a Man who is suffering as we have never seen a man suffer." They reasoned, "This Man must have committed the most terrible sins the world has ever known, and God is punishing Him." They were like the comforters of Job.

Isaiah 53:4 (*KJV*) says, "Surely he hath borne our griefs, and carried our sorrows: yet we did esteem him stricken, smitten of God, and afflicted." That phrase "we did esteem him" means w*e regarded Him* or *we looked upon Him* as someone "stricken, smitten of God, and afflicted." That's the way the world looked upon Jesus. They thought, *Here* *is a Man smitten of God. God is dealing with Him in judgment.*

But the world was wrong. Jesus didn't die for His sin, nor did He die for the sin of the Father or of the Holy Spirit. The very next verse is a contrasting verse, and it tells us the truth: "But he was wounded for our transgressions, he was bruised for our iniquities: the chastisement of our peace was upon him..." (v. 5 *KJV*).

The punishment that secures our peace with God was upon Jesus, "...and with His stripes we are healed." That entire verse ought to be in the first person. In fact, if you want a deeper revelation in your heart of what Jesus did for you in His redemptive work on the Cross, memorize Isaiah 53 and put it in the first person: *"But He was wounded for MY transgressions. He was bruised for MY iniquities. The punishment that secured MY peace was upon Him and by His stripes, I am healed!"*

"Were you there when I crucified my Lord?"

Indeed, we *were* there at the Cross. You may say, "But the Cross happened 2,000 years ago, and I'm living 2,000 years later!" That's no problem with God, any more than it is a problem for Him to save you today even though Jesus died 2,000 years ago. You *were* there at the Cross, just as I was. Even if you go to hell, you were there.

Anyone who goes to hell will have to live forever with the knowledge that Jesus bore his sins and went to hell *for* him so he wouldn't have to. I think that the height and the consummation of a person's hell will be the realization that he is there and that he didn't have to be there, to know that Jesus purchased a ticket to Heaven for him and he refused to pick it up. He insisted on going to hell, even though Christ had already paid the price.

Jesus has suffered our guilt, our sin, and our hell. He was wounded for our transgressions; He was bruised for our iniquities. That is the way to look at it, the *only* way to look at it.

Who killed Jesus? The great God of Heaven, knowing there was no other way for man, predestined His death before the foundations of the world. The great God of Heaven delivered Jesus over to the enemy to be killed for only one reason-because of the sin within the human race.

There would have been no Cross, had there been no sin. There would have been no sin, had there not been man. And there is not a person alive today who was not at that Cross. Not a one. I was there at the Cross, and so were you.

Just suppose you could go to Jerusalem and find the hammer that drove the nails into the flesh of Jesus. Suppose you could put the handle of that hammer under a microscope and see the fingerprints on that hammer. If that microscope revealed the true spiritual meaning of what you were looking at, you'd see your own fingerprints on the handle of that hammer.

Our hands are bloody. We are guilty. We're not just guilty of human error or of doing something slightly wrong as man would see it. Rather, we are guilty of making it necessary for the Son of God Himself to go to the Cross and die for us.

But this one act of Jesus is our only hope, for He went there for you and for me. Knowing that Jesus died on the Cross for mankind, how could we think that we cannot be forgiven? And if we are forgiven, how could we believe that He doesn't continue to forgive us? Since we know that God predestined the death of Christ on our behalf before the world even began and that God delivered Jesus to Calvary by the hands of the Jews and the Romans, how could we do anything but believe that God will also save *us* to the uttermost as we trust in Him?

I say to you today that this is all that the Cross is-God's great love message, declaring to us that He was pleased to offer His Son because of His great love for us.

And today God says to *you*: "I want to stand in your place, I want to take your sin and your punishment. I want to take your hell. All you have to do is come to Me and receive the wonderful gift of forgiveness and eternal life that is yours through Jesus, My Son."

For Further Information

For additional copies of this book
or for information regarding
Dr. Bill Bennett's ministry schedule,
please write:

Dr. Bill Bennett
104 King Arthur Drive
Wilmington, NC 28403

email: <u>bill.bennett@mentoringmen.org</u>

Please include your prayer requests and comments when you write.

www.ingramcontent.com/pod-product-compliance
Lightning Source LLC
Chambersburg PA
CBHW060539100426
42743CB00009B/1578